Who Makes the Law

Who Makes the Law
The Supreme Court, Congress, the States, and Society

TIMOTHY D. CHENEY

Linfield College

Prentice Hall
Upper Saddle River, NJ 07458

Library of Congress Cataloging-in-Publication Data

Cheney, Timothy D.
    Who makes the law : the Supreme Court, Congress, the states, and
  society / Timothy D. Cheney
        p.   cm.
    Includes bibliographical references and index.
    ISBN 0-13-493081-9 (paper)
      1. Legislative power—United States.   2. Legislation—United
  States.   3. Constituent power—United States.   4. Exclusive and
  concurrent legislative powers—United States.   5. Judge-made law—
  United States.   6. United States.   Supreme Court.   I. Title.
    KF4930.C48   1998
  328.73'077—dc21   97–41066
                                                                        CIP

Editorial production/supervision
  and interior design: Mary Araneo
Editorial director: Charlyce Jones Owen
Editor in chief: Nancy Roberts
Acquisitions editor: Michael Bickerstaff
Editorial assistant: Kathryn Sheehan
Marketing manager: Christopher DeJohn
Buyer: Bob Anderson
Cover designer: Patricia Wosczyk

This book was set in 10/12 New Baskerville by A & A Publishing
Services, Inc., and was printed and bound by Courier Companies, Inc.
The cover was printed by Phoenix Color Corp.

 © 1998 by Prentice-Hall, Inc.
Simon & Schuster/A Viacom Company
Upper Saddle River, New Jersey 07458

Printed in the United States of America
10   9   8   7   6   5   4   3   2   1

ISBN 0-13-493081-9

Prentice-Hall International (UK) Limited, *London*
Prentice-Hall of Australia Pty. Limited, *Sydney*
Prentice-Hall Canada Inc., *Toronto*
Prentice-Hall Hispanoamericana, S.A., *Mexico*
Prentice-Hall of India Private Limited, *New Delhi*
Prentice-Hall of Japan, Inc., *Tokyo*
Simon & Schuster Asia Pte. Ltd., *Singapore*
Editora Prentice-Hall do Brasil, Ltda., *Rio de Janeiro*

To Justice B.Z.O.

Contents

Preface

The intent of this book is to provide a general framework on the relationship between the the Supreme Court, Congress, the states, and society regarding the creation and implementation of laws. It does not delve into the role of the executive branch. The book uses some cases for illustration. During the preparation, and since the completion of this book, other cases on issues considered in this book have been heard. Further laws have been enacted. The law is constantly evolving and active. Hopefully, after reading this book, you will have a better idea of the process and the rationale behind the actions of the the Court, Congress, the states, and society as they try to create and implement the law.

ACKNOWLEDGMENTS

Sherie Dulaney provided invaluable assistance in reading and rereading this book as it moved through its drafts. Leslie McKay helped enormously in making this book more coherent and reader friendly. Many thanks to both of them. I'd also like to thank the following Prentice Hall reviewer's for their input: Elmer E. Cornwell, Jr. of Brown University and Bonita A. Sessing-Matcha of Hudson Valley Community College.

Who Makes the Law

Introduction

We the People of the United States, in Order to form a more perfect Union, establish Justice, insure domestic Tranquility, provide for the common defense, promote the general Welfare, and secure the Blessings of Liberty to ourselves and our Posterity, do ordain and establish this Constitution for the United States of America.

Preamble to the Constitution of the United States

THE LAW

The libraries are filled with volumes filled with laws. There are federal, state, county, and local laws. There are both federal and state constitutions. The typical lawyer's office has walls filled with law books. Many of these law books are seldom, if ever, read by the lawyers in whose offices the books line the shelves. So, why do we have so many laws? What are the reasons, what are the purposes?

Laws reflect societal goals. What society wants to accomplish, or prevent, is reflected in its laws. At the time of passage, every law had some coherent reason. As society changes, so too do the laws change. This can be illustrated by the appearance in newspapers of humorous laws that remain on the books long after their practical applicability. For example, now and again you may see a law making it illegal to ride a horse into a saloon. For most people, that seems quite silly. However, when it was originally adopted, there may have been a certain number of folks who would have been inclined to ride their horses into saloons. (For those who have been to rodeo days in some parts of the country, those laws may still appear to be valid!)

The law attempts to be fair, to be just. In order to be fair to everybody, the law may seem a bit unfair to everybody. All of us can't do whatever we want. In order to establish and promote justice, the law provides certain guidelines for conduct; it sets at least minimum standards which must be followed. Many of these guidelines are designed to maintain a certain amount of order. Basically, the law attempts to regulate relationships among individuals, and between individuals and society. The idea of regulating relationships in a manner for the greater good of society is a constant throughout the study of law.

WHY LAWS CHANGE

Laws are primarily guidelines for behavior. They reflect societal goals and notions of right and wrong. It is important to understand, however, that the law does not compel the best in us; instead, it attempts to prevent the worst in us. There is this constant tension in the law; we wish to balance the concept of individual freedom with the greater interest of the general society. The law merely provides some minimum standards in this regard.

The laws will change to reflect society's mood. In that regard they are something like a pendulum, swinging back and forth. Some areas of law are more fluid than others. For instance, criminal laws tend to be more fluid in terms of what's a crime, what's the punishment, what are the procedures to be followed. In understanding this idea, it is helpful to consider how the law is written, interpreted, and enforced:

> Written by federal and state legislative bodies (How strict are the guidelines for our conduct?)
>
> Interpreted by the courts (Are terms given a narrow or broad interpretation?)
>
> Enforced by the executive branches of government—and by society itself (How aggressively are the laws actually enforced?)

Each of these areas may change as society sees fit at a particular time. This idea will be raised throughout this book. For now, let's consider laws relating to driving under the influence of alcohol as an example of how the laws change to adapt to society's mood. Everybody hates "drunk driving." Therefore, the laws change. They change in how they are written, interpreted, and enforced:

> *How they are written:* The presumption of "under the influence" drops from .15 to .08 blood alcohol content. This makes the guidelines more strict. The penalties are also increased, which acts as an incentive for compliance with the laws.
>
> *How they are interpreted:* Concepts of "duty" are interpreted more broadly which means bartenders, social hosts, and possibly even companions may be liable for the actions of drunk drivers. This may encourage third parties to watch out for others.

How they are enforced: There may be roadblock checks, saturation patrols, and so forth. The increased enforcement works as an incentive for compliance since violators are more likely to get caught and punished.

This all reflects societal attitudes at the time.

WHO HAS FINAL SAY?

The question often arises: Who does have the final say on matters of law? Who has the power? Does the Supreme Court? The Congress? The executive? The states? Or, do "We the People"? Ultimately, it may be about the balance of power between the interested parties and the answer may come down to:

Who will exercise the power?

What is the proper role of each party under the Constitution?

Who will protect individual/minority interests from the power of the majority?

Does the Constitution provide protection from a particular governmental action?

Does the Constitution provide for an expansion of rights?

Part of the equation here really is "Who takes the heat?" Many of the issues are controversial and it may be easier for the nonelected official (the justices) to take the heat, since they do not have elective pressures. For instance, it may be difficult for a legislator to vote against a law banning flag burning, given the nature of the political process and the ability of a political opponent to turn that vote into a sound bite indicating the legislator is un-American. This becomes an issue for the states since many state court judges are subject to such elective pressures. Political pressure can also be seen in matters involving abortion rights, prayer in schools, and similarly emotional concerns.

These are some of the issues we will address in this book as we consider decisions of the Supreme Court and the responses made by the various interested parties.

Note: We do see, in confirmation hearings for justices, these political pressures. They are supposed to dissipate once an individual has been confirmed.

OUTLINE OF THIS BOOK

This book will address the issue of who does have the final say by looking at various responses to Supreme Court opinions.

Chapter 1   The Supreme Court

We will start with some basic background on the Supreme Court, including the process and methods involved in selecting and deciding cases.

In 1803, Chief Justice John Marshall stated "It is emphatically the province and duty of the judicial department to say what the law is." (**Marbury v. Madison;** see Chapter 1.) While that principle set forth nearly 200 years ago remains true, it seems increasingly evident that the Supreme Court may not *always* have the final say. Congress, individual states, and society may not always follow the lead of the Court. Also, sometimes the Court, by the manner in which the justices "say what the law is," does not do a very good job of setting forth any unambiguious guidelines for others to follow.

There may be instances where the Court refuses to act on an issue. This may involve basic constitutional limitations, an (occasional) act of deference to another branch, or a simple refusal to hear a lower court case appeal.

Chapter 2   Amending the Constitution

If Congress disagrees with a constitutional interpretation by the Court, it may attempt to alter that decision by amending the Constitution. Attempts have been made in recent times regarding school-prayer and flag-burning decisions. Given the difficulty of the amendment process, these attempts, while of temporary social and political interest, are generally unsuccessful.

Occasionally, Congress may attempt to amend the Constitution to solidify, or at least respond to, a directive from the Court. This sort of amendment effort might be seen regarding the issue of term limitations for elected officials.

Chapter 3   Congressional Legislation

If Congress disagrees with a statutory interpretation by the Court, it may attempt to alter that decision by enacting new legislation.

Recent examples of this include the **Grove City College** case, which gave a restrictive reading to Title IX of the Educational Amendments of 1972, a federal law requiring gender equity in educational institutions receiving federal funds. Congress responded by enacting the Civil Rights Restoration Act, which clearly set forth that Title IX applies to any institution receiving federal assistance and a violation of law in any program can result in the loss of federal funds. The Civil Rights Act of 1991 was in direct response to a series of court decisions in 1989 involving job discrimination. The Religious Freedom Restoration Act of 1993 was in direct response to **Employment Division v. Smith** (1990), a case involving the sacramental use of peyote. The Flag Protection Act of 1989 was in direct response to the first flag-burning case, **Texas v. Johnson**. (Later, after the second case, **U.S. v. Eichman** (1990), the amendment attempt failed.)

These situations are of continuing interest because the Court will often accept a subsequent case which deals with the new legislation. Sometimes the Court will restate its position, as it did in **Eichman,** when it threw out the Flag Protection Act as unconstitutional. Sometimes the Court will nod towards Congress as it did in **Franklin v. Gwinnet** (1992) when it stated: "In seeking to correct what it considered to be an unacceptable decision on our part in Grove City. . . . We cannot say . . . that Congress has limited the remedies available to a complainant [Author's note: A "complainant" is the party who brings the legal action.] in a suit brought under Title IX." In that case the Court rendered an interpretation of Title IX which it felt was in keeping with what *Congress* said the law was. Situations involving interpretations of federal law and the intent of Congress may involve a continuing dialogue between the Court and Congress. This is a more common situation, since the Court is generally reluctant to hold acts of Congress *unconstitutional,* although, as the Flag Protection Act case shows, the Court can and will exercise that power on occasion.

Occasionally, Congress may act to solidify an opinion of the Court through further legislation. This can be seen in the Equal Access Act, which provides certain access to schools for religious groups.

There may be instances where Congress doesn't act, or doesn't provide details, and leaves that chore to the Court. This can occur when there are difficult definitional issues involved, and it would be problematical to attempt, in legislation, to be overly precise. This can be seen in an area such as "sexual harassment."

Since there is a great deal of ongoing dialogue between these two branches, Chapter 3 will be longer—to let us track through a variety of issues.

Chapter 4   The States and Society

If states disagree with decisions of the Court, they may, to some extent, alter the impact of those decisions through their own laws or constitutions. States may provide more protection from governmental intrusions than is provided in the U.S. Constitution. For instance, in the peyote case mentioned above, the Court noted that some states did provide an exemption from their drug laws for such sacramental use. While such an exemption was permissible under the U.S. Constitution, the Court held that it was not required. This situation can also occur regarding certain forms of speech, which may be provided more protection under state constitutions.

Sometimes society itself may simply ignore pronouncements by the Court. Deeply held feelings concerning social issues will not suddenly change because nine robed figures in Washington render an opinion. This can be seen in a variety of areas such as school desegregation, gender equity, or school prayer. The result is that, unless enforcement occurs either by public agencies or private lawsuits, the ruling may remain without much impact.

Power and Deference

In large part the underlying issue here is power. Where does the power lie? Under the Constitution, the Congress writes the law, the Court interprets the law, and the executive branch enforces the law. The question often arises in a given situation as to who will *exercise* the power? When will one branch defer to another? Often, the Court will defer to legislative actions—through administrative agencies—when the issue is one of particularized expertise of an agency. However, as to matters of law and constitutional interpretation, the Court is highly unlikely to defer to anyone.

An exhaustive study of this complex subject is not in the scope of this book. We will not get into the issues of "original intent," "strict constructionism," and the like. Like all terms relative to the Constitution, these terms are subject to a wide variety of interpretations. (It has been stated that if "strict constructionism" simply meant reading the words of the Constitution, the only qualification to become a Supreme Court justice would be the ability to read!) Our goals in this text are: to provide information illustrating the dialogue between the Court, Congress, the states, and society; to illustrate the problems and limitations of the process; and to spark discussion, debate, and consideration of the extraordinary challenge of protecting and accommodating the rights and interests of the individual *and* the community in a democratic society.

CHAPTER 1

The Supreme Court

The focus of this book is on the various responses to decisions by the Supreme Court. First, we need a bit of background on the Supreme Court, including its process of selecting and deciding cases.

THE CONSTITUTION OF THE UNITED STATES

Article III

Section 1. The judicial power of the United States, shall be vested in one supreme Court, and in such inferior Courts as the Congress may from time to time establish. . . .

Section 2. (2) In all Cases affecting Ambassadors, other public Ministers and Consuls, and those in which a State shall be a Party, the supreme Court shall have original Jurisdiction. In all the other Cases before mentioned, the supreme Court shall have appellate Jurisdiction, both as to Law and Fact, with such Exceptions, and under such Regulations as the Congress may make.

ROLE OF THE SUPREME COURT

The role of the Court is set forth in Article III of the Constitution. Compared to Articles I and II, which set forth the powers and duties of the Congress and the executive branches respectively, Article III is rather short. Originally, the Court was not seen as a supremely powerful force.

In 1803, the Supreme Court rendered its decision in **Marbury v. Madison.** The case involved the last-minute appointment of various judgeships by the lame duck Federalist president, John Adams. Having lost the election for president, as well as control of both houses of Congress, the Federalist Party hoped to maintain some control through these last-minute appointments. Some became known as "midnight judges," in reference to President Adams staying up late the night before the inauguration of Thomas Jefferson in order to complete as many appointments as possible. One appointee, William Marbury, did not receive his appointment prior to the inauguration, and James Madison, secretary of state for the new administration, refused to make the delivery of Marbury's commission as a justice of the peace.

Marbury brought suit under the Federal Judiciary Act of 1789, Section 13, which provided that suits to compel performance by a public official of their offical duties could be brought directly to the Supreme Court. The chief justice, John Marshall, was a Federalist and no supporter of the new Republican President Jefferson. It would've been logical to suppose that Marshall would find in favor of Marbury and compel the delivery of the commission.* However, the Court first had to consider the validity of the provisions of the Federal Judiciary Act of 1789. Those provisions, which enabled the Supreme Court to essentially act as a trial court would have to be constitutional for Marbury to have his case heard by the Supreme Court. The Court, with Marshall writing the opinion, held that part of the Act was not constitutional in that it granted more power to the Supreme Court than was intended by the framers and as was set forth in the body of the Constitution. Therefore, even though the Court agreed that Marbury had been wronged, the Court was without power to hear the specific case before it. That part of the opinion seemed to limit the power of the Supreme Court. However, in so holding, the Court solidified the principle of judicial review by which it does have the power to review acts of Congress. Marshall made this clear when he stated "It is emphatically the province and duty of the judicial department to say what the law is."

Marbury solidified the status of the Supreme Court and the role of judicial review. It acknowledged and affirmed the power of the Court to rule on the constitutionality of congressional actions. In later cases the Court held that it had that same power in relation to state courts, state legislatures, and the executive branch. Since the Supreme Court is the branch of government with expertise in constitutional law, there is a logic to this position.

While the principle set forth in **Marbury** nearly 200 years ago remains true, it seems increasingly that the Supreme Court may not always have the final say. This despite what Justice Robert Jackson stated in **Brown v. Allen** (1952): "The Court is not final because it is infallible; the Court is infallible because it is final." Congress, individual states, and society may not always follow the lead of the Court. Congress may amend the Constitution or enact modified legislation, states may enact modified legislation, or society may simply

---

*Compare this situation to **U.S. v. Nixon**, concerning the presidential tapes involving Watergate, where Chief Justice Burger, appointed by President Nixon and considered an ally, wrote the opinion of the Court compellng production of the tapes. He cites **Marbury v. Madison** in his opinion.

ignore the Court. Sometimes the Court, by the manner in which the justices "say what the law is" does not do a very good job of setting forth any guidelines for others to follow and this can often lead to further legislation or litigation.

Keep in mind that the role of the Court goes to the constitutionality, not the wisdom of laws. Justices periodically refer to this, as seen in the following cases. In **Griswold v. Connecticut** (1965), regarding a law banning the use of contraceptives, Justice Stewart stated in his dissent:

> I think this is an uncommonly silly law. . . . But we are not asked in this case to say whether we think this law is unwise or even asinine. We are asked to hold that it violates the United States Constitution. . . . And that I cannot do. . . . Courts do not substitute their social and economic beliefs for the judgment of legislative bodies, who are elected to pass laws. . . . We are here to decide cases agreeably to the Constitution and laws of the United States. "It is the essence of judicial duty to subordinate our own personal views, our own ideas of what legislation is wise and what is not."

Justice Scalia echoed these sentiments in **CTS Corp. v. Dynamics Corp.** (1987), when he stated: "Law can be both economic folly and Constitutional."

In **Immigration and Naturalization Service v. Chadha** (1983), Chief Justice Burger stated as his opening paragraph: "The fact that a given law or procedure is efficient, convenient and useful in facilitating functions of government standing alone, will not save it if it is contrary to the Constitution."

Making the point that the Court is ruling on the constitutionality and not the wisdom of a law involves politics, policy and public perception, all of which we will discuss when we consider the responses to Court opinions.

SELECTING THE CASES TO BE HEARD

Basic Constitutional Restrictions

There are some standard constitutional constraints observed by the Court which come under a general umbrella of "justiciability," meaning appropriate and capable of judicial resolution. Among these are the following:

1. cases and controversies
2. ripeness
3. mootness
4. political questions or policy questions/deference

Cases and Controversies

Article III, section 2, of the Constitution provides that federal courts have jurisdiction of "cases" and "controversies." This basically means the Court cannot, and will not, render a purely advisory opinion. There must be an actual, current, adversarial proceeding.

Ripeness

This is a logical part of the "cases" and "controversies" limitation. If a case is not "ripe," there hasn't been sufficient adversarial consideration of the issue. The Court will decline to address hypothetical future questions. For instance, if legislation is enacted banning "indecency" on the internet, an individual would be unable to go to court to obtain an order preventing enforcement against some information which had yet to be put on the internet.

Mootness

This is essentially the other extreme from "ripeness." When the issue in question has somehow reached resolution, there is no need for the Court to act. If it did act, it would be giving an advisory opinion, which we have seen it will not do.

Note: There may be an occasional exception to the barrier of mootness. Such was the case in abortion decisions (See **Roe v. Wade**) where, given the reality of the litigation time lines, the issue would never get heard otherwise since any woman raising the issue of state restrictions would have given birth long before the time the Court might hear the issue.

Political Questions

The Court states what the law is; that is its role under the Constitution. It is not a political body. Traditionally, the Court will not involve itself in "political questions." The question is open as to what constitutes a "political question."

In the famous reapportionment (establishing voting districts) case, **Baker v. Carr** (1962), the Court did decide what appeared to be a political question. The issue was the reapportionment of legislative districts in the Tennessee legislature. The residents of Tennessee who were challenging the apportionments wanted the matter heard in federal court. They felt the state courts were not responsive to their concern that the failure to reapportion the state legislature left too much power in rural areas and did not properly reflect the current population realities of urbanization. Justice Brennan, in attempting to set forth guidelines for what is and isn't a political question, considered some of the following factors:

> whether there was "a constitutional commitment of the issue to a coordinate
>   political department,"

or,

whether there was "an impossibility of deciding without an initial policy determination of a kind clearly for nonjudicial discretion,"

or,

whether the Court ruling would display a "lack of respect due coordinate
branches of government,"

or,

whether there was the "potentiality of embarrassment from multifarious pronouncements by various departments on one question."

The Court held, by a 6-2 vote, that the particular issue could be heard.

As we go through the examples in this book, keep Justice Brennan's language in mind and decide for yourself whether it is always clear and/or followed. We will see that when the Court sets forth tests or guidelines for decision making, the elements of the tests themselves may remain open to dispute
and legitimate differences of opinion as to their interpretation.

Policy Questions/Deference

There may be other cases which, if not specifically a "political question,"
the Court still feels are better left to other branches of government because
the matter is either legislative in nature or does not involve any constitutional
issue. As noted above, this may call for subjective decisions to be made. Justices
may disagree as to what is a "political question," or something to be left to the
legislative (or executive) branch. The Court will often note that it is an issue
to be settled by the legislative branch, either at the state or federal level. One of
the ongoing tensions occurs when the Court determines *it* is the one to decide,
and the dissents then state that the matter would be better left to the legislative bodies (see Chapter 4).

Justice Powell in **Frontiero v. Richardson** (1973), an equal protection case
involving certain benefits available to military personnel, (see Chapter 2), stated:

> It seems to me that this reaching out to preempt by judicial action a major polit-
> ical decision which is currently in process of resolution does not reflect appro-
> priate respect for duly prescribed legislative process. There are times when the
> Court, under our system cannot avoid a Constitutional decision on issues which nor-
> mally should be reached by the electoral representatives of the people. But demo-
> cratic institutions are weakened, and confidence in the restraint of the Court is
> impaired, when we appear unnecessarily to decide sensitive issues of broad social
> and political importance at the very time they are under consideration within the
> prescribed Constitutional processes.

In **United Steelworkers v. Weber** (1979), the issue before the Court was whether Title VII of the Civil Rights Act of 1964 prevented a private affirmative action plan. The Court upheld the plan, but Justice Burger in dissent noted:

> The Court reaches a result I would be inclined to vote for were I a member of Congress considering a proposed amendment of Title VII. I cannot join the Court's judgment, however, because it is contrary to the explicit language of the statute and arrived at by means wholly incompatible with long established principles of separation of powers.

In his dissent, Justice Rehnquist noted:

> . . . our duty is to construe rather than rewrite legislation.

This case illustrates a division on the Court over whether it was appropriate for the Court to take any action. It was not the first time, nor the last, that such a division has occurred.

Sometimes it seems that the Court sidesteps issues to an extent. They may rule that a particular right exists under the Constitution, but that the parameters are left to the legislative bodies. This has been seen in the issue of abortion, where the Court ruled there is some sort of right to an abortion, but has also noted that states and Congress may place certain restrictions on that right. (The Court has upheld many such restrictions while still maintaining the essential right to an abortion per **Roe,** see Chapters 3 and 4.)

In **Employment Division v. Smith** (1990), a case in which a state refused unemployment benefits to a Native American who had been fired for using peyote as part of a religious ceremony, Justice Scalia stated:

> It may fairly be said that leaving accommodation to the political process will place at a relative disadvantage those religious practices that are not widely engaged in; but that unavoidable consequence of democratic government must be preferred to a system in which each conscience is a law unto itself or in which judges weigh the social importance of all laws against the centrality of all religious beliefs.

[You might compare this sentiment with that of Justice Jackson in **West Virginia v. Barnette** (1943), a case we will hear more of later, in which he noted some things are beyond the vote.]

After **Smith**, Congress did legislate to essentially offset the refusal of the Court to protect certain religious freedoms (Religious Freedom Restoration Act). Some states also enacted legislation to protect the religious activities.

Questions to Consider: Will legislative bodies always act in such a manner? Is it the role of the Court to protect minority interests from the possible tyranny of the majority?

Other Instances of Deference

The Court may defer to the expertise of certain administrative agencies regarding their particular area of technical expertise. This may occur when the question is clearly within the area of legislative expertise of the agency. However, if the issue is one of legal or constitutional definition, the Court will not defer, which is consistent with their role as the expert on matters of law.

A sort of deference, or at least refusal to act, occurred in the baseball antitrust case, **Flood v. Kuhn** (1972). In that case the Court noted that since Congress had not responded to the judical creation of an antitrust exemption for baseball, there wasn't anything for the Court to do. This opinion contains the interesting language that the antitrust exemption for baseball is an aberration but since it is a long standing one, it isn't for the Court to act. The Court stated:

> The aberration is an established one.

The Court noted the inaction of Congress as well.

> Remedial legislation has been introduced repeatedly in Congress but none has ever been enacted.
>   It [the Court] has voiced a preference that if any change is to be made, it come by legislative action that, by its nature, is only prospective in operation.

The Court basically wants Congress to end the antitrust exemption enjoyed by baseball. Many commentators feel that since the exemption was created by the Court, it is for the Court to remove it. The Court might get that opportunity sometime. Congress does not seem inclined to remove it, although, with the recent labor problems with "America's favorite pastime," Congress has been discussing the issue.

The Court Will Hear or Refuse to Hear the Case

The Court does not have to hear every case. There is no right to "take it all the way to the Supreme Court." Unless specifically provided by the Constitution, cases are heard when the Court grants a writ of certiorari. The term is Latin meaning "to be informed." A writ may be granted in response to a petition for such a writ. Granting the writ means the Court will hear the case and later issue a full written opinion.

The Court may issue per curiam ("by the court") opinions which are decisions of the whole Court. These are generally unsigned and without any individual opinions. They tend to be brief and to summarily dispose of an issue.

(Occasionally, per curiam opinions are rendered in response to major issues, but that is rare.)

There are no strict guidelines for the issuance of a writ of certiorari ("writ of cert," granting "cert" are terms often used). Rule 10 of the Rules of the Supreme Court of the United States says:

> A review on writ of certiorari is not a matter of right, but of judicial discretion, and will be granted only when there are special and important reasons therefor."

Generally, the chances of having the writ granted are better if the matter involves legal error of a constitutional nature, an issue of Federal law, or there is a conflict in the lower courts. Still, there are no hard and fast rules.

The primary informal rule is what is known as "the rule of four." For the Court to agree to grant the writ and hear the case, four justices have to be in favor. The theory seems to be that if four justices feel the question is important enough, the full Court should hear the matter. They are not making a decision on the merits at this point; they simply agree to hear the case.

The result of this process is that the Court refuses to hear many appeals of lower court decisions. There are approximately 5,000 petitions every year. Only a small percentage are granted. In the 1994 Term, for example, the Court issued less than 100 full opinions.

The impact of such a refusal is that the lower opinion stands, and has precedential impact in the particular jurisdiction where it was heard. Beyond that, it does not signify any ruling or opinion of the Supreme Court. This is important to keep in mind since there are times when a refusal to grant the writ gets a great deal of publicity, and it may appear that the Court is making a ruling on the specific merits of the case. That is not the case.

A BIT OF HISTORY/THE COURT PACKING PLAN

Presently, the Court has nine members. There are eight associate justices and one (first among equals) chief justice. The Constitution does not set forth the precise number of justices, and there have been as few as five and as many as 10. Since 1869 the number has been steady at nine.

However, there was one point in time when the size of the Court was very much at issue. In February 1937, President Franklin Delano Roosevelt sent to Congress the Judicial Reorganization Bill. This legislation called for the appointment of one new justice for every sitting justice who was over the age of 70. There were six such justices at that time. While presented as a means of lessening the work load of the justices, this "Court Packing Plan" was designed to enable Roosevelt to achieve his New Deal, by creating a Court more friendly to his legislative goals.

The New Deal involved a great deal of federal legislation involving wages, hours, and other labor and social issues. Congress had passed the legislation, but the Supreme Court had held the legislation as invalid because the Congress lacked the constitutional authority to pass such laws. The core legal issue was whether the Congress had the power, under the Commerce Clause of the Constitution, which provides Congress with the power "To regulate Commerce . . . among the several States." The Court took a narrow view and interpretation of the Commerce Clause and held in numerous cases that matters of wages, hours, and labor issues were local and did not involve "interstate commerce." Therefore, the Congress could not regulate in that manner. Roosevelt wanted a Court which would be more inclined to take a broad view of the Commerce Clause and therefore find congressional authority.

The proposed legislation created quite a political uproar, but it was short lived. In March, 1937, the Court decided **NLRB v. Jones & Laughlin Steel Corp.** in which they upheld the enactment of the National Labor Relations Act of 1935 (The Wagner Act), thereby holding that Congress did have broad power under the Commerce Clause. As a result, the New Deal legislation moved ahead, and the Court Packing Plan never went forward. It does remain as an historical reminder of the tension existing between the executive and judicial branches, some of which can occasionally be seen whenever the executive disagrees with a Court opinion.

THE CURRENT SUPREME COURT

Justice	Date	Appointed by
Rehnquist	1/7/72, 9/26/86 (as Chief)	Nixon
Stevens	12/19/75	Ford
O'Connor	9/25/81	Reagan
Scalia	9/26/86	Reagan
Kennedy	2/18/88	Reagan
Souter	10/9/90	Bush
Thomas	11/1/91	Bush
Ginsburg	8/10/93	Clinton
Breyer	7/29/94	Clinton

At this point (1997), six of the justices have been appointed in the last eleven years. (Seven of the sitting justices were nominated by a Republican President and two by a Democrat. This book will not discuss the "political" nature of appointments.) Even more significantly, since the Robert Bork defeat in 1987, the appointments have tended to be more centrist. That is, with the exception of Clarence Thomas, who is seen as a "conservative," the justices been less likely to take positions seen as extremely "conservative" or "liberal." (In the case of Thomas, there were certainly myriad other issues: replacing Thurgood Marshall, Anita Hill's testimony, his comments regarding never having debated **Roe v. Wade**, etc.)

Rather than look to make broad statements concerning the law, these newer justices are seen as more likely to be incremental in their thinking. That is, they will move slowly and piece by piece on an issue, and are unlikely to render broad opinions. Justice Scalia would be the major exception to this method of operation, with his desire for broader rulings. This Court is more inclined to render opinions dealing strictly with the case and facts at hand, rather than be more sweeping and attempt to create clear all-purpose rules. For instance, they are more inclined to look at specific requirements regarding obtaining an abortion and decide whether those specific requirements are constitutional. Others would rather decide either: 1. **Roe** should be overturned, or 2. Any restrictions are unconstitutional. This case by case approach tends to result in fact-specific rulings which do not provide much in the way of general guidance as to the law. If in fact the law is designed so that individuals can plan and project their actions to be in accordance with the law, this narrow case by case method can create uncertainties and continuing litigation.

This centrist (not considered strictly "conservative" or "liberal") group generally (not always in agreement) includes Kennedy, Souter, Ginsburg and Breyer. It may also include O'Connor. Kennedy and O'Connor might be classified as more conservative centrists and Ginsburg and Souter perhaps as more liberal centrists. Breyer may be a bit of both. The exception from recent nominees (since 1987) is Thomas who is solidly in the conservative group which also includes Scalia and Rehnquist. The one justice who, on some issues could conceivably be classified as a "liberal," but more accurately would be classified as "independent," is Stevens. Stevens did file the most dissents in the 1994 Term, which may reflect the trend toward conservatism of the Court as much as his point of view. There appears to be no true "liberal" on the current Court in the sense of William Brennan or Thurgood Marshall.

There remains the overall question of the identity of the Court. About the only certainties are Scalia and Thomas. Recently, Rehnquist has not been with them on all cases, although he remains with them on most issues. This may indicate a slight shift into a bit of isolation for Scalia, and may be, in part, a function/result of the ascerbic nature of his opinions. It's difficult to change people's minds when you treat them as not having one. It will be interesting to see how Scalia responds in the event he becomes at all isolated. When Justice Brennan was isolated on the liberal end he was still effective. In reality, with the Court becoming more conservative and Thomas voting with Scalia 90 percent of the time in the 1994 Term, Scalia is unlikely to find himself isolated. While extreme positions on the Court may be unable to build consensus for that particular point of view, they may be able to shift the center a bit because more moderate views may then appear more reasonable by way of contrast. As discussed below, vigorous dissents may also work to lessen the immediate impact of a decision in that they may lessen the sense that the issue has been finally resolved.

THE COURT OPINIONS

The Court is the one branch of government which issues written justifications and explanations for its actions and decisions. In terms of generating public support for a decision, the written opinions of the Court can prove helpful by setting forth clear reasons and rationales. However, as we will see, there are also obstacles to generating support for the decisions. This involves factors of timing, ruling, length and clarity of decisions, broad guidelines vs. case-by-case analysis.

Timing. The gap between the date of oral argument and the decision is often seen as an indication of how strongly the Court feels about the issues raised. A quick opinion generally indicates there was little disagreement on the outcome. This doesn't seem to happen often. The Court opens its session on the first Monday in October. An argument comes before the Court, there is sometimes lots of publicity, and then several months pass before an opinion is issued. While part of this delay is inherent in the process, ideological divisions on the Court lead to extended delays as the justices wrestle with the issues and attempt to reach an agreement on an acceptable opinion.

Ruling. Certainly the 9-0 rulings carry more force than those which are 5-4. Often, if the opinion is 9-0, the opinion will be issued more quickly. Also, with total agreement, the opinion may be more short, clear and forceful. There are also no dissents to set forth opposition. Increasingly, the Court seems fragmented in its decision making. While the justices are in agreement a good percentage of the time; approximately 40 percent of their opinions over the last three terms (1992/93, 1993/94, and 1994/95) have been unanimous, either with one opinion or a majority opinion with concurring opinions, they also seem increasingly divided on many issues. Over the last three terms nearly 20 percent of the Court opinions have been by a 5-4 vote. This is reflective of genuine disputes in society and the Court regarding the issues as well as interpretation of the Constitution. However, when the Court is this fragmented regarding emotionally charged issues (death penalty, religion, abortion, affirmative action, etc.), it is difficult for a society to discern much in the way of guidelines.

Length and clarity. A short clear opinion is generally indicative of a strong clear consensus of the Court, which the Court hopes will more readily serve as a guideline for society. [Sometimes, even short, 9-0 opinions may not do much in terms of public response. See **Brown v. Board of Education** (1954). Short and 9-0.] Increasingly, instead of short, clear opinions, these fragmented (5-4) rulings lead to lengthy, detailed, and complex opinions. Additionally, it often seems as if each justice wants to have a say. This leads to opinions along the lines of: "I concur with Parts I, III, V and VII of the Court's opinion, but dissent as to the other parts." Or, "I concur with Parts II and VI, but dissent with Parts III, IV and VII." In such circumstances, where there is little consensus or clarity on the Court, there can be limited impact on the society. The public is simply not able to comprehend what was said. The media is stuck with trying to cram the long, detailed, fragmented opinions into a sound bite.

An example of this sort of opinion and its impact is the **Regents of the University of California v. Bakke** (1978) case involving affirmative action. In a very long and complex set of opinions, the Court seemed to say that race could be one factor in determining admissions to medical school. With no clear majority on the legal issues, the result has been uncertainty and a stream of subsequent cases. (Consider how many cases involving affirmative action the Court has heard over the years, and whether anybody has a clear understanding of the issue.) These plurality opinions, in which there is no majority agreement as to the legal basis for the judgment, have increased in recent years, and this tends to lessen the force of the Court's opinions.

Part of the problem in this area is often due to the rather fine legal points being at issue. Below we will discuss matters such as the level of review for a law, "strict scrutiny," "compelling governmental interests," and so forth. When opinions are based on what appears to be legalese, it increases the difficulty for the public. Often, the public may feel that the opinions are nothing more than lawyers writing for other lawyers. There may be some validity to this criticism. Since the justices rarely see or know about the individuals involved in the cases they hear it is often easy for them to be in a legal vacuum where these fine and somewhat obscure points of law dominate the process.

Broad guidelines or case-by-case analysis. Some justices (e.g., Antonin Scalia) would rather draw bright lines on issues, while others don't find that either possible or desirable (e.g., Sandra Day O'Connor). Many of the issues that most interest the public tend to be difficult in terms of establishing clear distinct guidelines, therefore creating confusion. This is often the situation in cases requiring the Court to define terms such as "sexual harassment," "establishment of religion," "obscenity," and the like. Society is often left with judicial statements along the lines of "I can't define it, but I know it when I see it," which one Justice said of obscenity/pornography. While perhaps the best that can be hoped for, it's not terribly helpful in terms of influencing our attitudes or acting as a guideline for our conduct. The fall 1993 **Harris v. Forklift Systems** case regarding sexual harassment is an example where even Justice Scalia, who is probably the justice most in search of clear rules, admitted difficulty regarding defining sexual harassment.

These days the Court is often seen as a sort of trial court, focusing on the specific facts of the case before it and how the law may apply to those specific facts. This particularized, fact-specific approach offers little in the way of general guidance due to the variety of possible factual situations which can arise. (Often, the best the Court can do is create some general "tests," to help determine the outcome. We will see this more in Chapters 3 and 4.) This case by case, fact-specific handling of cases tends to lessen the value of the opinions as precedent. Precedent, or "stare decisis," ("let the decision stand") means the Court, and all lower courts will generally follow the previous ruling of the Court when faced with the same factual situation. The concept of following precedent provides stability, consistency, and predictability, which inspires faith in the law. Precedent may not be followed where historical conditions have changed, the previous case was wrongly decided as a matter of law, or a grave injustice would occur. Since the present Court tends to be more fragmented (leading to more plurality opinions) and very case specific (leading to less precedential value of the opinion), the dialogue between the Court, Congress, the states, and society will continue, since it is less likely that final answers have been established.

Note: A unique feature of the Court in our democratic society is its non-democratic nature. Since the Court is often called upon to protect the Constitutional interests of those in the minority, it is not necessarily ruling with the majority of the population in those instances where it may be protecting against the "tyranny of the majority." The Bill of Rights provides certain individual protections, such as freedom of speech and freedom from unreasonable search and seizure, which may not always suit the general public (see **West Virginia v. Barnette** in Chapter 2). This aspect of the Court's role will be noted regarding Congress and the states, where legislators may sometimes, in deference to the realities of elective politics, take stands which they may well know the Court will find unconstitutional. An example would be in the Flag Protection Act.

CHAPTER 2

Amending the Constitution

THE CONSTITUTION OF THE UNITED STATES

Article V

The Congress, whenever two-thirds of both Houses shall deem it necessary, shall propose Amendments to this Constitution, or, on the Application of the Legislatures of two-thirds of the several States, shall call a Convention for proposing Amendments, which, in either Case, shall be valid to all Intents and Purposes, as part of this Constitution, when ratified by the Legislatures of three-fourths of the several States, or by Conventions in three fourths thereof, as the one or the other Mode of Ratification may be proposed by the Congress; Provided that no other Amendment which may be made prior to the Year One thousand eight hundred and eight shall in any Manner affect the first and fourth Clauses of the Ninth Section of the first Article; and that no State, without its Consent, shall be deprived of its equal Suffrage in the Senate.

Congress may respond to Court opinions in a variety of ways. We will see in Chapter 3 that Congress may enact new legislation if part of a law, or a specific interpretation of a law, has been ruled unconstitutional. When the Court has ruled that a state law is unconstitutional, Congress might first attempt to frame a federal law which would be held constitutional. (See the Flag Protection Act discussion below.) A more drastic response is to enact a constitutional amendment to override the opinion. Since the Court does have the final say as to the constitutionality of a law, Congress generally will not attempt further specific legislation where the Court has ruled a federal law is totally unconstitutional. However, by changing the Constitution to explicit provide for certain types of legislation (for example, laws prohibiting flag burning), Congress can remove the ability of the Court to declare such laws unconstitutional.

The Court has traditionally been reluctant to hold federal laws in toto unconstitutional. The more common situation is for the Court to provide an interpretation of the law with which Congress might disagree. That will often lead to further federal legislation, as discussed below in Chapter 3.

The amendment process, set forth in Article V of the Constitution, is difficult. The most common method is the process which requires a two-thirds vote by each house of Congress followed by ratification by three- fourths of the states. All but the Twenty-first Amendment have been adopted in this manner. (The Twenty-first Amendment was adopted by special convention in three-fourths of the states. It repealed the Eighteenth Amendment—Prohibition.)

There are currently twenty seven amendments to the Constitution. The Bill of Rights makes up the first ten. In over two hundred years, there have been only seventeen further amendments. A review of the amendments makes it clear that amendments have been enacted to deal with issues of governance (voting rights, legislative requirements, etc.) rather than social issues. The glaring exception would be the Eighteenth Amendment, Prohibition (ratified January 29, 1919). The "success" of the social issue amendment is amply illustrated by the enactment of the Twenty-first Amendment, which repealed it (ratified December 5, 1933). The problem regarding amendments on social issues is that unless they address a fairly universally agreed upon concept and definition (e.g., involuntary servitude), it is problematic to put something into the Constitution which is specific to the particular times, when the Constitution is designed to be flexible and adaptable for all times. For instance, a right of "privacy" could perhaps be placed into the Constitution directly (as it is in some state constitutions) because the term itself is somewhat vague and adaptable. However, providing or denying a right to an "abortion," might not be as subject to interpretation and therefore would not afford such flexibility. This point will be elaborated upon below regarding attempts to amend the Constitution regarding abortion, school prayer, and so on.

The difficulty of the process itself, and the reluctance to use the amendment process for social issues, has restricted this avenue for Congress to overturn Supreme Court decisions they do not like. It has not, however, kept them from trying—and occasionally succeeding.

HISTORICAL EXAMPLES

There have been a few instances where Congress has been successful in amending the Constitution in direct response to rulings of the Court. As noted, these generally dealt with matters of governance rather than social issues.

1. **Chisholm v. Georgia** (1793). This case involved the jurisdiction of federal courts to hear cases brought by citizens of one state against another state. The Court found such jurisdiction existed. The Eleventh Amendment, passed by Congress in March, 1794, and ratified in January, 1798, provides:

The judicial power of the United States shall not be construed to extend to any suit in law or equity, commenced or prosecuted against one of the United States by citizens of another State, or by citizens or subjects of any foreign State.

2. Scott v. Sandford (1857) (The "Dred Scott Case"). The Court denied Congress the power to exclude slavery from the territories, and basically held that blacks couldn't be citizens. This decision is obviously not considered one of the Court's finer moments.

The Thirteenth Amendment, passed by Congress in February, 1865, and ratified in December, 1865, provides:

Neither slavery nor involuntary servitude, except as punishment for crime whereof the party shall have been duly convicted, shall exist within the United States, or any place subject to their jurisdiction.

The Fourteenth Amendment, passed by Congress in June, 1866, and ratified in July, 1868, provides:

All persons born or naturalized in the United States, and subject to the jurisdiction thereof, are citizens of the United States and the State wherein they reside. No State shall make or enforce any law which shall abridge the privileges or immunities of citizens of the United States; nor shall any State deprive any person of life, liberty, or property, without due process of law; nor deny to any person within its jurisdiction the equal protection of the laws.

These amendments did involve governance, as well as social matters.

3. Pollock v. Farmer's Loan and Trust Co (1895). This case held the federal income tax to be unconstitutional. The Sixteenth Amendment, passed by Congress in July, 1909, and ratified in February, 1913, provides:

The Congress shall have power to lay and collect taxes on incomes, from whatever source derived, without apportionment among the several States, and without regard to any census or enumeration.

4. Oregon v. Mitchell (1970). The Court invalidated an Act of Congress giving 18-year-olds the right to vote in State as well as Federal elections. The Twenty-sixth Amendment, passed by Congress in March, 1971, and ratified in July, 1971, provides:

The right of citizens of the United States, who are eighteen years of age or older, to vote shall not be denied or abridged by the United States or by any State on account of age.

Other amendments have been passed and ratified at least in part due to holdings of the Court which denied rights to various groups.

The Nineteenth Amendment (1920) provides voting rights for women, an historically excluded class. There were several cases denying voting rights, as well as other rights, for women which in part provided an impetus for this amendment.

The Twenty-fourth Amendment (1964) outlawed poll taxes, which were used historically to exclude traditionally excluded groups from the governing process. A 1937 Supreme Court case had upheld the constitutionality of a state poll tax.

RECENT AMENDMENT ATTEMPTS

In recent years, particularly in the last year or so, there appears to be a bit of amendment fever as efforts have been made to amend the Constitution in response to decisions involving abortion, school prayer, and flag burning. In the session beginning in January, 1995, there have been more than 140 proposals for amendments to the Constitution. Most of the proposals don't make it to the floor for a vote of the full body. However, Congress did vote on amendments regarding term limits, a balanced budget, and flag desecration. To date, none of these attempts has been successful. We will now consider a few specific amendment efforts involving abortion, prayer in school, flag burning, and term limits. Note that of these four, only one—term limits—relates more to governance than social matters.

Abortion

Background and Court Opinions. There are no express guarantees of a right to abortion or to privacy contained within the Constitution. The 1965 **Griswold v. Connecticut** case set the stage for **Roe v. Wade** (1973), by "finding" a constitutional right of privacy in the Constitution. Justice Douglas found this right in the "penumbras" of various provisions of the Bill of Rights. This meant that while the right was not expressly stated, it was basically implied by virtue of the other express provisions of the Constitution.

In his opinion, Justice Douglas, after noting that many specific rights are not mentioned in the Constitution, but are included, went on to say:

> . . . specific guarantees in the Bill of Rights have penumbras, formed by emanations from those guarantees that help give them life and substance. . . . Various guarantees create zones of privacy.

He went on to specifically note the First, Third, Fourth, Fifth and Ninth Amendments.

That case certainly helped set the stage for Justice Blackmun's opinion in **Roe**, where he stated:

> The Constitution does not explicitly mention any rights of privacy. In a line a decisions . . . the Court has recognized that a right of personal privacy, or a guarantee of certain areas or zones of privacy, does exist under the Constitution. . . . These decisions make it clear that only personal rights that can be deemed "fundamental" or "implicit in the concept of ordered liberty" . . . are included in this guarantee of personal privacy. . . . This right of privacy . . . is broad enough to encompass a woman's decision whether or not to terminate her pregnancy. We, therefore, conclude that the right of personal privacy includes the abortion decision, but that this right is not unqualified and must be considered against important state interests in regulation.

This last language, while establishing the right to abortion, also left room for legislative action to address "important state interests." As a result, the extent of the right of privacy regarding abortion has remained somewhat vague and debated both in and out of the courts. (See Chapters 3 and 4.)

Social Note: The particular times of these two opinions (1965 and 1973) may well have influenced the justices. The mid-'60s were a time of questioning authority and sentiments favoring personal autonomy. By 1973, the issue of women's rights was at the forefront with the passage of the Equal Rights Amendment (adopted by Congress on March 22, 1972, and ratified by 22 of the necessary 38 states by the end of the year; for more on the ERA, see Chapter 3). While the Supreme Court is ideally supposed to remain above the politics of the day, they are individuals and cannot remain totally removed from political and social realities. In Chapter 4 we will discuss how society responds to Court opinions. However, keep in mind that society can influence opinions, at least to some extent. Certainly, society influences the legislative responses as legislators respond to elective pressures.

Congress: Several attempts to amend the Constitution in response to **Roe** have been made.

In 1974 and 1975, hearings were held in a Senate subcommittee, but no proposal came out.

In 1982 a proposal to allow the states to regulate abortion was voted down by a vote of 50 to 49.

In 1983 an amendment to restrict or outlaw abortion "failed" by a vote of 50 to 49, meaning that while it passed, it did not receive the necessary two-thirds majority required to amend the Constitution.

To date, no abortion amendment proposal has been successful but, considering the emotional and political nature of the issue, it is almost certain that future attempts will be brought forth. As noted earlier, one obstacle to such an amendment is that it could be considered "social" in nature and, if set forth with clarity in the Constitution, might not allow for adaptation to the particular time.

Prayer in Public Schools

Background and Court Opinions: Prayer in public schools has a long history of legislative and judicial activity. Predominately, the Supreme Court has ruled against state attempts to provide for prayer in public schools, holding that it violates the establishment clause of the First Amendment. The Court wrestles with the First Amendment dictates which address both establishment of religion and its free exercise. The First Amendment provides:

> *Congress shall make no law respecting an establishment of religion, or prohibiting the free exercise thereof. . . .*

A brief listing of the major cases is as follows:

In 1962, in **Engel v. Vitale**, the Supreme Court ruled that a prayer, written and authorized by the state, could not be used in the public schools. The prayer stated "Almighty God, we acknowledge our dependence upon Thee, and we beg Thy blessings upon us, our parents, our teachers and our Country."

The Court held that such a prayer in public schools constituted a promotion of religion and essentially coerced all students to adhere to a religious doctrine. The purpose of the establishment clause in the First Amendment is not to eliminate religion from public life, but to prevent the promotion of any particular view. Where there is a semblance of coercion, such as in a public-school setting where students have no choice but to be in attendance, publicly sponsored religion is not permissible.

In 1980, in **Stone v. Graham**, the Court held it was improper to post the Ten Commandments in the public schools pursuant to a State law.

In 1983, in **Abington School District v. Schempp**, the Court disallowed state-mandated prayer or devotional readings in the public schools.

In 1985, in **Wallace v. Jaffree**, the Court disallowed a state mandated moment of silence for "meditation or voluntary prayer."

In 1992, in **Lee v. Weisman**, the Court disallowed school-sponsored prayer at graduation ceremonies.

However, in the same year, a lower court permitted "nonsectarian and nonprostelyzing" prayer at a high school graduation as long as it was initiated by a student and approved by a majority of the graduating class. The Supreme Court declined to review this decision, leaving some major doubt as to the issue. In 1995, the Court dismissed a case on the issue of prayer at graduation due to mootness because the students involved had graduated. It seems likely the Court will revisit this issue. (See Chapters 3 and 4 for further discussion and developments in this area.)

Congress: Congress has reacted to the decisions of the Court with attempts at amending the Constitution to provide for the allowance of school prayer. Literally hundreds of amendments have been proposed. To date, none has been adopted by Congress. Among the efforts have been the following:

Senate 1966: Failed by 9 votes.

House 1971: Failed by 28 votes.

Senate 1984: Failed by 11 votes.

By "failed" I mean the vote was short of the required two-thirds majority. At this writing, the most recent proposal, "The Religious Freedom Amendment," is being discussed in the House of Representatives.

Note: West Virginia v. Barnette, a 1943 case involving compulsory salute of the flag, contains some language which may be applicable to this and other areas we will address. In that case, Justice Robert Jackson stated:

The very purpose of a Bill of Rights was to withdraw certain subjects from the vicissitudes of political controversy, to place them beyond the reach of majorities and officials and to establish them as legal principles to be applied by the Courts. One's right to life, liberty and property, to free speech, a free press, freedom of worship and assembly, and other fundamental rights may not be submitted to vote; they depend on the outcome of no elections.

He went on to state:

But freedom to differ is not limited to things that do not matter much. That would be a mere shadow of freedom. The test of its substance is the right to differ as to things that touch the heart of the existing order. If there is any fixed star in our constitutional constellation, it is that no official, high or petty, can prescribe what shall be orthodox in politics, nationalism, religion or other matters of opinion or force citizens to confess by word or act of faith therein.

Remember that the role of the Court is in part to protect against the possible tyranny of the majority. In that sense it is not "democratic," since it may be preserving rights of those in the minority rather than always upholding majority rule. Recall Justice Scalia's comments in the Introduction.

The point is that, with a diverse society, with a huge variety of religious beliefs; any majority vote on the issue of religion would not protect those religions with smaller numbers of members. The Constitution is designed to protect individual belief and to prevent those who may not be in the majority from feeling somehow out of the sphere of protection. The Court will attempt to prevent the government from appearing to endorse any particular religion. (See Justice O'Connor's language in **Lynch v. Donnelly** (1984) in Chapter 3.)

Flag Burning

Background and Court Opinions: The First Amendment has always been a source of debate over its meaning. While the amendment is written in absolute terms "Make no law" abridging freedom of speech, there are recognized exceptions to that, such as the classic case of shouting "fire" in a crowded theatre. "Speech" itself has been broken down into various categories such as "commercial speech" (advertising). An even more difficult matter is what constitutes "symbolic speech?" "Symbolic speech" is certain forms of nonverbal expression which convey a message, such as wearing an armband as a form of political protest. While most speech is protected, conduct is not. Where is the line? Political speech tends to be most favored as it seems to be most in keeping with the intent of the framers to allow for full and open political discourse.

Issues regarding freedom of speech come to the Supreme Court as well as lower federal courts in many forms. In recent years there have been cases regarding hate speech, speech codes on college campuses, obscenity, rights to exclude groups from marches and many more. At the core of these cases is the difficulty of finding a proper accommodation between the competing interests of a robust public discourse and individual rights with that of a harmonious community. These are not easy issues and the emotion involved adds to the difficulty. A full discussion of that is beyond the scope of this book, but many of these issues and difficulties are present and illustrated in the flag burning cases.

Texas v. Johnson (1989). At the 1984 Republican Convention, Johnson burned a U.S. flag as part of a political protest. A state law made it a crime to intentionally or knowingly desecrate the flag and Johnson was convicted under that law. In a 5-4 decision the Court ruled that the law was unconstitutional in that it was a restriction on speech. The Court found that burning the flag in the manner Johnson did was "speech." The Court also found the law was not content neutral in that it was aimed at the content of the speech, which in this case was political in nature. The Court will be more protective of forms of speech when the subject matter is political. The Court noted that the bedrock principle of the First Amendment right to freedom of speech is that the government may not dictate the content of speech and cannot restrict speech just because it doesn't agree with the speaker.

The (sometimes uncomfortable) role of the Court was noted by Justice Kennedy in his concurrence when he stated:

> The case before us illustrates better than most that the judicial power is often difficult in its exercise. We cannot here ask another branch to share responsibility, as when the argument is made that a statute is flawed or incomplete. For we are presented with a clear and simple statute to be judged against a pure command of the Constitution. The outcome can be laid at no other door but ours.

The hard fact is that sometimes we must make decisions we do not like. We make them because they are right, right in the sense that the law and the Constitution, as we see them, compel the result. And so great is our commitment to the process that, except in the rare case, we do not pause to express distaste for the result, perhaps for fear of undermining a valued principle that dictates the decision. This is one of those rare cases.

Justice Kennedy clearly wrestled with the impact of the decision. He did not in any way favor burning a flag, but he recognized the larger principle of protecting what he felt was constitutionally protected speech.

Recall Chapter 1 regarding court opinions. The justices are not unaware of the impact of their rulings. When they know the opinion may not be popular, they may attempt to soften the blow by inserting language explaining why they are compelled to reach their decision. In terms of getting the public to "buy in" to the decision, this may be counterproductive. Much like strongly worded dissents, lukewarm, almost apologetic opinions and concurrences can have the same effect on reducing the impact of an opinion as any sort of guideline for conduct or beacon of authority.

Congress: At the urging of President George Bush (who had used the flag salute issue to get elected), Congress enacted the Flag Protection Act in 1989. The Court addressed that issue in **U.S. v. Eichman** (1990), (see Chapter 3) and tossed out the federal law. In response to that, in 1990, Congress started a move to amend the Constitution to allow for laws to prevent desecration of the flag. Since subsequent amendments to the Constitution take precedence over previous amendments, this proposed amendment would have essentially altered the First Amendment to the extent that it dealt with flag burning as speech. The proposed amendment failed.

One of the difficult issues in drafting any amendment regarding flag burning is that of definitions. What does "speech" mean? What does "desecrating the flag" mean? Consider examples on uses of the flag you may have seen. On clothing and other personal items. What uses honor the flag and what uses may desecrate the flag? These problems of definition and impact are often a major obstacle for amendments which are "social" or "moral" in nature. As we noted earlier, most amendments have dealt with matters of governance and political process.

Note: One of the problems with "reactive" laws (laws which are intended to cover a particular situation) is that they have unintended consequences and wind up covering situations not intended or foreseen. These flag burning cases started with a political protester, who might have otherwise remained anonymous. There was no epidemic of flag burning.

See Chapter 3 for more on Congress enacting legislation to counter a Court opinion. It is interesting to note from the following sequence of dates how quickly the process moved with the flag at issue:

Texas v. Johnson June 1989

Flag Protection Act September-October 1989

United States v. Eichman June 1990

Amendment effort June 1990

In 1995, as a result of the Republican Party's takeover of the House, the issue of flag burning was back. An amendment was proposed and passed the House. The Senate version, which provided "The Congress shall have power to prohibit the physical desecration of the flag of the United States," failed by three votes to obtain the required two-thirds majority. At this writing, no amendment has been approved, but it does not mean the issue has gone away.

Term Limits

Background and Court Opinions: In the 1990s there has been rising dissatisfaction with "professional politicians," and the "throw-the-bums-out" cry has been heard with frequency. One method attempting that has been the movement for term limits. Many states have enacted term limits for state politicians, and some states attempted to limit federal congressional terms as well.

In **U.S. Term Limits Inc. v. Thornton** (1995), the Supreme Court held that states could not, constitutionally, limit the terms for U.S. congresspersons. The Court also noted that congressional legislation could not do so either because Congressional terms of office are established in the Constitution. This does set up the possibility of Congress attempting to amend the Constitution, not necessarily to counter the decision of the Court, but to follow their lead regarding how to accomplish the goal of term limits. Whether Congress will support an amendment to limit their terms is an open question.

In reaching their conclusion, the Court stated:

> We are, however, firmly convinced that allowing the several States to adopt term limits for congressional service would effect a fundamental change in the constitutional framework. Any such change must come not by legislation adopted either by Congress or by an individual State, but rather—as have other important changes in the electoral process—through the Amendment procedures set forth in Article V. . . . In the absence of a properly passed constitutional amendment, allowing individual States to craft their own qualifications for Congress would thus erode the structure envisioned by the Framers. . . .

The opinion noted the following constitutional provisions. Amendment Seventeen (1913) (direct elections of senators); Amendment Nineteen (1920) (extending suffrage to women); Amendment Twenty-two (1951) (presidential term limits); Amendment Twenty-four (1964) (prohibition against poll taxes); Amendment Twenty-six (1971) (lowering age of voter eligibility to eighteen).

Congress: To date, there has been a great deal of discussion regarding term limits, but no amendment has been passed.

Note: Sometimes, there is a drive to amend the Constitution to force society or its legislators to do that which is already within their power. Term limits do exist; voters can vote out the incumbents. A balanced budget can be obtained; the politicians have to have the courage and ability to compromise. Sometimes, it seems easier if we are forced to do that which we might already be able but, for various reasons, be incapable or unwilling to do.

IMPACT OF THE AMENDMENT PROCESS ON COURT OPINIONS

The Court, in reaching decisions, is aware of the amendment process. Sometimes, the existence of an amendment in process may have an impact on the Court, with its thinking being that the amendment will resolve the issue. An example might be the Equal Rights Amendment (ERA), which in 1972 passed Congress by the necessary two-thirds. Twenty-eight of the necessary thirty-eight states fairly quickly ratified the amendment. With this progress being made, the Court had some reluctance to act on matters of gender equity.

For instance, in **Frontiero v. Richardson** (1973) Justice Powell concurred in the judgment, which held that administrative convenience was not sufficient reason to hold that spouses of male Air Force officers were automatically considered dependents but that spouses of females would have to prove dependency—but refused to join Justice Brennan in holding that classification based upon sex "like classification based upon race, alienage and national origin are 'inherently suspect and must therefore be subjected to close judicial scrutiny'."

He based his refusal to do so in part on the following:

> There is another, and I find compelling, reason for deferring a general categorizing of sex classifications as invoking the strictest test of judicial scrutiny. The Equal Rights Amendment, which if adopted will resolve the substance of this precise question, has been approved by the Congress and submitted for ratification by the States. If this Amendment is duly adopted, it will represent the will of the people accomplished in the manner prescribed by the Constitution. By acting prematurely and unnecessarily, as I view it, the Court has assumed a decisional responsibility at the very time when state legislatures functioning within the traditional democratic process, are debating the proposed amendment.

Justice Brennan, in his opinion, saw matters differently.

> Congress itself has concluded that classifications based upon sex are inherently invidious, and this conclusion of a coequal branch of Government is not without significance to the question presently under consideration.

Note: This difference of opinion regarding the standard to be applied to classifications based upon sex led to a plurality decision regarding the standard, which eventually evolved into an "intermediate scrutiny" standard. (See Chapter 3 for further discussion on this issue of the appropriate level of scrutiny.)

The legislative side of this issue was that many legislatures felt that since the Court was essentially providing the rights to be established constitutionally by the ERA, there was no need for the ERA. The history of the ERA is a good example of the difficulty of the amendment process, as well as the sometimes confusing nature of the dialogue between the branches of government. In the next chapter, we will discuss that dialogue.

Sometimes, when an attempt at an amendment fails, legislatures, state and federal, will attempt revised legislation to work around Supreme Court decisions, or in hopes that the Court may reconsider an issue. Sometimes, when the Court has ruled that the Constitution does not compel a certain result, but also does not prevent it, then legislative bodies may attempt legislation to provide for such rights. (This will be discussed in more detail in Chapters 3 and 4.)

CHAPTER 3

Congress Legislates

THE CONSTITUTION OF THE UNITED STATES

Article I

Section 1. All legislative Powers herein granted shall be vested in a Congress of the United States. . . .
Section 8. (1) The Congress shall have the power . . . (3) To regulate Commerce . . . among the several States. . . .

There are instances when Congress will legislate to counteract an opinion of the Supreme Court. Sometimes, Congress will enact legislation to solidify or enhance an opinion. Occasionally, Congress will remain silent, even when the Court may seem to invite it to take some action (recall the **Flood** case).

The situations which arise due to the constitutional or legislative interpretation provided by the Court tend to be the most interesting since they often involve a continuing dialogue between the Court and Congress. This dialogue is apparent in both the court opinions and the legislation. As noted earlier, the Court's role is to determine the constitutionality of legislation as well as to interpret the law. They do not rule on its wisdom or advisability.

As Justice Douglas stated in his opinion in the **Griswold** case:

> We do not sit as a superlegislature to determine the wisdom, need and propriety of the laws that touch economic problems, business affairs or social matters.

However, as we have seen, where this line between the judicial and the legislative functions is drawn can be difficult to ascertain.

LEGISLATION TO COUNTER OPINIONS OF THE COURT

We will examine this dialogue between the Court and Congress in cases where Congress legislates to counter opinions of the Court in the following situations:

Regarding federal law, we will consider issues of gender including pregnancy and Title IX. We will also consider some of the issues involved with flag burning. Regarding state laws we will consider issues of abortion, religion, and flag burning. The issues to be addressed are often emotional. The following discussion is not intended to be exhaustive. It is intended to illustrate the nature, and perhaps limitations, of the dialogue between the Court and Congress on these issues. In Chapter 4, we will address the responses of states and society.

FEDERAL LAWS

The Court will render, generally speaking, one of several kinds of decisions:

Totally tossing out a federal law. This does not happen often. It has occurred approximately 125 times in our history, but only a few times since 1937, when the Court gave a broad interpretation of the Commerce Clause in the **Jones & Laughlin** case. (Recall from Chapter 1 regarding the Court interpreting the law in a broad or narrow manner, a narrow interpretation of the Commerce Clause led to the Court Packing Plan.) The Court generally acknowledges the basic power of Congress to enact legislation itself, but may dispute the constitutionality of the particular act, or may somehow limit, or expand, its application by virtue of the interpretation given to it by the Court.

However, in 1995, in **United States v. Lopez**, the Court did strike down a federal law as being beyond the scope of congressional power. The case involved the Gun-Free School Zones Act of 1990, which provided penalties for possession of guns near schools. The legal question for the Court was whether or not the Congress had the power to enact such legislation under the Commerce Clause. The wisdom or intention of the act was not an issue. The Court held that the issue of guns near schools was a local matter and therefore did not affect interstate commerce so as to provide for federal authority under the Commerce Clause.

Chief Justice Rehnquist, in his majority opinion, stated:

The Act neither regulates a commercial activity nor contains a requirement that possession be connected in any way to interstate commerce. We hold that the Act exceeds the authority of Congress "(t)o regulate Commerce . . . among the several States. . . ." U.S. Const., Art. I., Section 8, cl 3.

He went on to state, citing an earlier Court opinion:

Just as the separation and independence of the coordinate branches of the Federal Government serves to prevent the accumulation of excessive power in any one branch, a healthy balance of power between the States and the Federal Government will reduce the risk of tyranny and abuse from either front.

He also noted **Jones & Laughlin** and its impact.

Jones & Laughlin Steel . . . ushered in an era of Commerce Clause jurisprudence that greatly expanded the previously defined authority of Congress under the Clause.

Chief Justice Rehnquist pointed out that Congress had not established, on the record, the connection between possession of guns near schools and interstate commerce. The dissent felt there was such a connection, once again illustrating that intelligent people can view the same facts and circumstances and reach different results. The issue of Congress providing enough justification or evidence of its power may be critical to the further resolution of this issue, and will most certainly be raised in subsequent cases when they are heard by the Court.

Many people felt this case signalled a bit of a retreat from the deference the Court has granted to Congress regarding the basic power to enact legislation, even if the legislation appears to be local in nature (see Chapter 4 discussion on federalism). However, in a subsequent case, **U.S. v. Robertson** (1995), the Court, in a per curiam opinion issued less than a week later, held that operating a gold mine in Alaska did have a sufficient connection to interstate commerce in order to justify federal regulation. Recently, a Circuit Court of Appeals held that a federal carjacking law was constitutional. In another situation, one lower court held that the federal "Deadbeat Dad" law was beyond the power of the Congress under the Commerce Clause. Another lower court held the other way. In June, 1997, the Supreme Court invalidated provisions of the federal Brady Bill, which required state officials to conduct background checks on gun buyers, holding that such provisions exceeded the power of Congress (**Printz v. U.S.**, **Mack v. U.S.**). For many people, this seemed to confirm the retreat from deference to congressional action.

Interpreting a federal law in a manner with which Congress does not agree. An example of this occurred in 1989 when the Court interpreted the Civil Rights Act of 1964 in a manner with which Congress did not agree. There were a series of cases requiring an interpretation of the 1964 law regarding employment discrimination. When Congress found itself in disagreement with the interpretation of the law, they wrote a new law, the Civil Rights Act of 1991, to correct what they perceived as a misreading of the prior law. The matter of giving the law a broad or narrow interpretation is at issue in this context as well.

Interpreting the constitution in a manner with which Congress does not agree. The Court does not toss out a law, but notes that the Constitution does not compel a particular treatment or result, perhaps noting that it is for the legislative body to act. For instance, on the issue of "equal protection of the laws" under the Fourteenth Amendment, the Court was often called upon to interpret that clause as it relates to the rights of women. The issue was often whether the Constitution prevents certain treatment or laws, or compels laws to equalize treatment in all instances. From the end of the Civil War to 1971, in every case regarding the applicability of the equal protection clause of the Fourteenth Amendment to gender, the Court held it did not apply. Some of the language of the various Justices is quite fascinating. In **Bradwell v. Illinois** (1873), a case involving a woman's right to become an attorney, Justice Bradley, in concurring that Equal Protection is not applicable, stated :

> Man is, or should be, the woman's protector and defender. The natural and proper timidity and delicacy which belongs to the female sex evidently unfits it for many of the occupations of civil life.
>
> The paramount destiny and mission of women are to fulfill the noble and benign offices of wife and mother. This is the law of the Creator.

In somewhat less stark terms, this attitude seemed to more or less prevail until the early 1970s when, in cases which put men at a disadvantage, the Court started to find that perhaps gender discrimination was subject to equal-protection analysis.

Gender: General Issues

As indicated above, the Court has often struggled with the issue of gender (sex) as it relates to the Constitution, federal, and state law. This history is far beyond the scope of this book involving myriad laws, social policy, custom, etc. We will address a few particular issues. We will use the term "gender discrimination" when discussing "sex discrimination."

Standard of review. In gender discrimination cases, the issue often may be the standard of review which the Court applies to a law. If there is a "suspect" classification, the standard of review is "strict scrutiny" to establish a "compelling governmental interest." "Suspect" generally means there is some obvious characteristic or trait (race), a historical disadvantage, and obvious deprivation based upon the classification (slavery). "Strict scrutiny" is the highest, most exacting level of review the Court can use and it is often difficult for any law to withstand such a review. "Strict scrutiny" requires that the law fulfill a "compelling governmental interest" which is a very high standard and generally difficult to prove. (The issue of "compelling governmental interest" also arises in regard to "free exercise of religion" cases, which we will discuss below.) If there is not a "suspect" classification, the law must simply have a "reasonable basis rationally related to a legitimate governmental purpose." That standard is very easy to meet, particularly since the Court will give great deference to legislative judgments.

In cases involving gender, no majority of the Court has held gender to be a suspect classification requiring strict scrutiny of the specific law at issue. However, the Court has established an intermediate scrutiny area which requires "an important governmental interest" to justify a law based upon classification by gender.

Part of the problem in arriving at the proper standard regarding gender relates to the passage of the Civil Rights Act of 1964 (CRA) in which the classification of "sex" was added at the last minute in an attempt to defeat the legislation. The basic classification with which Congress was concerned was race. As a result of sex (gender) being added to the legislation at the last minute, there was little discussion of the matter of discrimination based upon sex and therefore there is almost no legislative history for the Court to review to assist them in interpreting the intent and meaning of the law. Also, as noted in Chapter 1, the Court declined some opportunities to act in this area while the Equal Rights Amendment was in process. There may well also be some historical baggage concerning the status of women in this society. Consider that it was not until the Twentieth Amendment, adopted in 1920, that women were provided with the right to vote under the Constitution.

Pregnancy

Background. As noted, "sex" was added to the Civil Rights Act of 1964 at the last minute, so there is no legislative record. This lack of a legislative record also relates to sexual harassment as a form of sex discrimination, which we will discuss later.

Continuing Dialogue between the Court and Congress
Court: **Geduldig** 1974
      General Electric Co. 1976

Congress: Pregnancy Discrimination Act 1978

Court: **Newport News Shipbuilding and Dry Dock Co.** 1983

Court: Geduldig v. Aiello (1974). The Court held that it did not violate equal protection if pregnancy benefits were denied under a disability plan. A major issue was the standard of review to be applied (recall above). The majority (Stewart, joined by Burger, White, Blackmun, Powell, and Rehnquist) held to the lesser (reasonably related) standard while the dissenters (Brennan, Douglas, and Marshall) wanted the higher (strict scrutiny) standard. In a footnote designed to show there was no gender bias present, Justice Stewart stated:

The lack of identity between the excluded disability and gender as such under this insurance program becomes clear upon the most cursory analysis. The program divides potential recipients into two groups—pregnant women and nonpregnant persons.

In **General Electric Co. v. Gilbert** (1976), the Court held that it was not a violation of Title VII of the Civil Rights Act of 1964 to fail to cover pregnancy related disabilities. In that case, Justice Rehnquist, writing for the majority, put the footnote of Justice Stewart into the main body of the opinion. Justice Stevens, in his dissent, mildly points out that a reasonable person might see such categorization another way.

Congress: The Pregnancy Discrimination Act 1978 (PDA) amended the CRA to expressly provide that discrimination based upon pregnancy is not allowed. Congress noted that the purpose of the Act was as follows:

To amend title VII of the Civil Rights Act of 1964 to prohibit sex discrimination on the basis of pregnancy. (10/31/78)

Court: In Newport News Shipbuilding and Dry Dock Co. v. EEOC (1983), the Court had to address the meaning of the PDA. They held that the pregnancy limitation in a health plan discriminated against male employees in that it provided less extensive pregnancy benefits for spouses of male employees than those provided female employees.

Justice Stevens, writing for the Court, stated at the start of his opinion:

In 1978 Congress decided to overrule our decision in General Electric Co. v. Gilbert 429 US 125 (1976), by amending Title VII of the Civil Rights Act of 1964 "to prohibit sex discrimination on the basis of pregnancy."

Later in the opinion he stated:

When Congress amended Title VII in 1978, it unambiguously expressed its disapproval of both the holding and reasoning of the court in the Gilbert decision. . . . The House Report stated: "It is the committee's view that the dissenting Justices correctly interpreted the Act." Similarly, the Senate Report quoted passages from the two dissenting opinions, stating that they "correctly express both the principle and the meaning of title VII."

In dissent, Justice Rehnquist states that he feels the Court is misreading the Pregnancy Discrimination Act. The facts of the case, with the issue revolving around a spouse of an employee, were such that Justice Rehnquist felt the act didn't extend as far as did the majority.

Note: It is interesting that the person bringing the action to seek to prevent an inequality of treatment on the basis of gender was a man. This has often been the case in gender discrimination litigation.

Gender Equity in Education

Background: In order to assure equality of opportunity, Congress passed The Educational Amendments Act of 1972, Title IX. The law provides that federal funds will be denied to any school which discriminates on the basis of sex.

The law is very short and has been open to interpretation. The Office of Civil Rights has issued some guidelines to attempt to clarify the requirements of the law. We will discuss this in more detail in Chapter 4.

Continuing Dialogue between the Court and Congress
Court: Grove City College v. Bell 1984

Congress: Civil Rights Restoration Act 1988

Court: Franklin v. Gwinnett 1992

Court: In **Grove City College v. Bell** (1984), the Court held that Title IX was violated only if the specific program receiving federal funds discriminated. This was a very narrow reading/interpretation of the law. The impact of this was that as long as a particular department—often the athletic department—didn't receive federal funds, it could discriminate without running afoul of the law.

Congress: Congress finally passed the Civil Rights Restoration Act of 1988. President Reagan vetoed the act, but Congress overrode that veto. Now, if an institution receives any federal funds, the entire institution is covered. Congress, in Section 2 of the Act, made certain findings.

The Congress finds that
(1) certain aspects of recent decisions and opinions of the Supreme court have unduly narrowed or cast doubt upon the broad application of title IX of the Education Amendments of 1972 . . . ; and
(2) legislative action is necessary to restore prior consistency and long-standing executive branch interpretation and broad, institutionwide application of those laws as previously administered.

Note: The act goes on to expressly note institutionwide application.

Court: In **Franklin v. Gwinnett** (1992), the Court held that a damages remedy is available for an action brought to enforce Title IX. Justice White stated:

In seeking to correct what it considered to be an unacceptable decision on our part in Grove City College v. Bell . . . Congress made no effort to restrict the right of action . . . or to alter the traditional prescription in favor of any appropriate relief for violation of a federal right. We cannot say, therefore, that Congress has limited the remedies available to a complainant in a suit brought under Title IX.

The Court here acknowledges the intent of Congress as to the broad interpretation to be given to Title IX.

Flag Burning

The issue of amending the Constitution to prevent desecration of the flag has been discussed in Chapter 2. Below, we will track the case history of the current issue and discuss both the state and federal law as well as the Court opinions.

STATE LAWS

Chapter 4 will briefly discuss the role of the states, issues of federalism and responses of the states and society to Court opinions. Here, we will focus on a Court opinion on a state law and the subsequent dialogue it generated between the Court and Congress.

Abortion

Background: As noted in Chapter 2, the issue of abortion rights is difficult, controversial, and could fill a book (or several). This discussion will be limited to illustrating the issue of dialogue between the Court and Congress. This dialogue illustrates the incremental nature of the Court (recall Chapter 1 regarding the Court opinions). In Chapter 4, we will follow up on the response of the states and society.

Continuing Dialogue between the Court and Congress
Court: Roe v. Wade 1973

Congress: Hyde Amendment

Court: Harris v. McRae 1980

Congress: 1995 Act regarding late term abortions

Court: Roe v. Wade (1973) threw out a Texas law which restricted the right to an abortion. The opinion spoke of many things and contained a variety of theories. (Recall Chapter 1 regarding the strength, clarity of opinions.) Justice Blackmun wrote (for a 7-2) Court:

> The Constitution does not explicitly mention any right of privacy. In a line of decisions, however, . . . the Court has recognized that a right of personal privacy, or a guarantee of certain areas or zones of privacy, does exist under the Constitution. In varying contexts, the Court or individual Justices have, indeed, found at least the roots of that right . . . in the penumbras of the Bill of Rights, Griswold v. Connecticut. . . .

> This right of privacy, whether it be founded in the Fourteenth Amendment's concept of personal liberty and restrictions upon state action, as we feel it is, or, as the District Court determined, in the Ninth Amendment's reservation of rights to the people, is broad enough to encompass a woman's decision whether or not to terminate her pregnancy.
>
> We, therefore, conclude that the right of personal privacy includes the abortion decision, but that this right is not unqualified and must be considered against important state interests in regulation.

That clause has opened the way for a variety of restrictions on the right to an abortion.

Congress: The Hyde Amendment. In federal legislation, including Title XIX of the Social Security Act, which is known as the "Medicaid" act, an amendment, now known as the "Hyde Amendment," after its sponsor, Henry Hyde, was added which provides:

> None of the funds provided by this joint resolution shall be used to perform abortions except where the life of the mother would be endangered if the fetus were carried to term; or except for such medical procedures necessary for the victims of rape or incest when such rape or incest has been reported promptly to a law enforcement agency or public health service.

The impact of this amendment was to essentially prevent the use of any federal funds for abortions.

Court: In **Harris v. McCrae** (1980) the Court stated:

> It is well settled that if a case may be decided on either statutory or constitutional grounds, this Court, for sound jurisprudential reasons, will inquire first into the statutory question. This practice reflects the deeply noted doctrine "that we ought not to pass on questions of constitutionality . . . unless such adjudication is unavoidable."

The Court recognized that:

> . . . we must consider the constitutional validity of the Hyde Amendment.

Justice Stewart, speaking for a five-justice majority, discussed their opinion in **Roe** and subsequent opinions, noting that **Roe** "protects the woman from unduly burdensome interference with her freedom to decide whether to terminate her pregnancy."

He went on to say:

> The Hyde Amendment . . . places no governmental obstacle in the path of a woman who chooses to terminate her pregnancy.

The Court rejected all other constitutional arguments against the Hyde Amendment. There were four justices who strongly dissented.

Congress: In the fall of 1995, Congress passed legislation banning a particular type of late term abortion. It is the first federal legislation since **Roe** which has banned any type of abortion procedure. President Clinton has indicated he will veto the bill. This could well lead to dialogue between the executive and congressional branches on this particular aspect of the issue.

Religion: Establishment Clause

Amendment I

Congress shall make no law respecting an establishment of religion, or prohibiting the free exercise thereof; . . .

Tension exists in the language of the First Amendment. The government shall not establish religion, nor shall it prohibit the free exercise. This apparent paradox, where the government must not engage in activities which seem to promote a particular religion, while at the same time not acting in a way that restricts anyone's religion, creates a constant stream of cases for the Court. In this part we will look at a few to illustrate the problems and the attempts at dialogue between the Court and Congress. In Chapter 4, we will look at some responses of the states and society.

Background: The role of religion in our society and the relationship between the government and religion is complex and constant. We hear of the "separation of church and state," but we're not sure what it means. We hear about the negative attitude towards religion in our schools, but we're not sure what that means. Again, we have an emotional issue, with deep feelings involved. We may look to the Supreme Court for some clarity, but we may not find it there.

Prayer in Public Schools. The issue of prayer in the public schools is ongoing. Recall the discussion in Chapter 2 and the series of cases heard by the Court and the legislative efforts as well as the efforts to amend the Constitution. In 1994, the Senate voted 93-7 to protect "constitutionally protected prayer" in schools. This bit of courageous legislation means—I'm not sure! It basically says "obey the law." It's the sort of legislation that makes Congress feel good, but doesn't add much to guide society. An amendment to this legislation which would've provided severe penalties was defeated, in part on the basis of schools not knowing what would be a violation.

As this issue remained in the forefront in 1995, President Clinton sent a memo to the secretary of education and the attorney general addressing the issue of religious expression in school. In that memo, he attempted to set forth the state of constitutional law as it relates to religious expression in schools. It is interesting to note that once the president clarified (or at least attempted to do so) the situation and status of the existing law, much of the clamor for a constitutional amendment died down, at least for the moment. This could in part relate to the issues noted in Chapter 1 regarding clarity of Court opinions and public dissemination and explanations by media and others.

Support, Promotion, Endorsement, or Accommodation. The question in these cases is where the line is drawn between accommodation, which allows for the free exercise of religion and,crossing over the line, promotion or endorsement, which would violate the establishment clause.

Continuing Dialogue between the Court and Congress

Court: In **Lemon v. Kurtzman** (1971), the Court attempted to set forth some guidelines, or a test, to determine when the establishment clause had been violated. The case involved state laws which allowed states to pay some teachers salaries and certain other educational costs of teaching nonreligious subjects in religious schools.

Chief Justice Burger, in the opinion for the Court, stated:

> Every analysis in this area must begin with consideration of the cumulative criteria developed by the Court over many years. Three such tests may be gleaned from our cases. First, the statute must have a secular legislative purpose; second, its principal or primary effect must be one that neither advances nor inhibits religion, . . . finally, the statute must not foster "an excessive government entanglement with religion."

These three criteria have become known as the "Lemon Test," for purposes of deciding whether a statute violates the establishment clause.

Justice Burger went on to say:

> Our prior holdings do not call for total separation between church and state; total separation is not possible in an absolute sense. Some relationship between government and religious organizations is inevitable. . . . Judicial caveats against entanglement must recognize that the line of separation, far from being a "wall," is a blurred, indistinct, and variable barrier depending on all the circumstances of a particular relationship.

If you think that language looks like "I can't define it, but I know it when I see it," you are not alone. As we have seen before, and will again, it is very difficult to set exact standards on some points of law. Consider how often in these areas the Court attempts to establish "tests," to guide themselves and others. It may be that by establishing a "test," the Court feels they can at least give the appearance of coherence and objectivity while saying what the law is and setting forth guidelines for our conduct. In Chapter 4 and the Conclusion, we will note and discuss some of these "tests."

Congress: Apart from political speeches about religion, family values, and calls for more religious values, Congress has been relatively quiet legislatively in this area. (See above.)

Religion: Exercise

Background: The other side of the First Amendment's religious protection is the guarantee of free exercise of religion. While this may seem clear enough, it often involves an analysis of the facts and circumstances to determine the limits of "exercise." Belief is fully protected. Actions are not. The problems arise when actions are held to be part of the belief. Trying to find where to draw this line is not unlike the situation involving "symbolic speech," such as burning a flag.

Continuing Dialogue between the Court and Congress

Court: In **Employment Division v. Smith** (1990), the Court held that Oregon's laws against the use of peyote, even in religious ceremony, did not violate the free exercise clause. As is often the result in these sorts of cases, the opinion was not unanimous and there were several long opinions and dissents.

Justice Scalia, in his opinion for the Court, stated:

> We have never held that an individual's religious beliefs excuse him from compliance with an otherwise valid law prohibiting conduct that the State is free to regulate. . . .
> . . . the right of free exercise does not relieve an individual of the obligation to comply with "valid and neutral law of general applicability on the ground that the law proscribes (or prescribes) conduct that his religion prescribes (or proscribes)."

In the majority opinion, Justice Scalia goes on to address the standard of review for any law which may impact religious conduct. In prior cases, which are noted by the Court, (**Sherbert v. Verner** (1963) and **Wisconsin v. Yoder** (1972)) the Court had held that any governmental action which substantially burdened a religious practice would have to be justified by a "compelling governmental interest." (Recall the level of scrutiny discussed regarding gender above.) Justice Scalia states that such a strict test is not appropriate in these cases, because it would allow for each individual to basically decide which general laws to obey.

Justice Scalia does note that a number of States have made exceptions for sacramental use of peyote. He finds that permissible, but not mandated by the Constitution or any federal law.

Justice O'Connor, in an opinion in which she concurs in the judgment but not in the reasoning, disagrees with part of Justice Scalia's opinion. She states:

> Although I agree with the result the Court reaches in this case, I cannot join its opinion.

She notes her disagreement with Justice Scalia's statements involving leaving the matter of the exemption to the legislative bodies. She states:

> Finally, the Court today suggests that the disfavoring of minority religions is an "unavoidable consequence" under our system of government and that accommodation of such religions must be left to the political process. Ante, at 890. . . . In my view, however, the First Amendment was enacted precisely to protect the rights of those whose religious practices are not shared by the majority and may be viewed with hostility. The history of our free exercise doctrine amply demonstrates the harsh impact majoritarian rule has had on unpopular or emerging religious groups such as the Jehovah's Witnesses and the Amish. Indeed, the words of Justice Jackson in West Virginia Bd. of Ed. v. Barnette (overruling Minersville School Dist. v. Gobitis) . . . are apt:
>
>> The very purpose of a Bill of Rights was to withdraw certain subjects from the vicissitudes of political controversy, to place them beyond the reach of majorities and officials and to establish them as legal principles to be applied by the courts. One's right to life, liberty, and property, to free speech, a free press, freedom of worship and assembly, and other fundamental rights may not be submitted to vote; they depend on the outcome of no elections.

After setting forth these thoughts, Justice O'Connor found there was a "compelling interest" for the State of Oregon to control peyote use in the manner set forth in their laws. Therefore, she was able to concur in the judgment.

Justices Brennan, Blackmun, and Marshall agreed with the first part of Justice O'Connor's opinion, and then parted company.

There was quite a lot of vocal response to the **Smith** opinion. While the Religious Freedom Restoration Act was going through the legislative process, the Court considered another free exercise case.

In **Church of Lukumi v. Hialeah** (1993), the Court held that city ordinances which seemed to target a particular religion's practices were invalid under the free exercise clause. At the time of that opinion, the Religious Freedom Restoration Act had not been signed into law, but was in process. The Court distinguished this case from **Smith.** They did not mention any pending legislation.

Congress: Congress did react to the **Smith** decision by passing the Religious Freedom Restoration Act of 1993. In that legislation, Congress set forth:

Findings:

The Congress finds that

(1) The framers of the Constitution, recognizing free exercise of religion as an unalienable right, secured its protection in the First Amendment of the Constitution;

(2) laws "neutral" towards religion may burden religious exercise as surely as laws intended to interfere with religious exercise;

(3) governments should not substantially burden religious exercise without compelling justifications;

(4) in Employment Division v. Smith 494 US 872 (1990) the Supreme Court virtually eliminated the requirement that the government justify burdens on religious exercise imposed by laws neutral to religion; and

(5) the compelling interest test as set forth in prior Federal Court rulings is a workable test for striking sensible balances between religious liberty and competing prior governmental interests.

(B) Purposes

The purposes of this chapter are—

(1) to restore the compelling interest test as set forth in Sherbert v. Verner, 374 U.S. 398 (1963) and Wisconsin v. Yoder, 406 U.S. 205 (1972) and to guarantee its application in all cases where free exercise of religion is substantially burdened; and

(2) to provide a claim or defense to persons whose religious exercise is substantially burdened by government.

In June, 1997, the Supreme Court held that Congress exceeded its powers in enacting the Religious Freedom Restoration Act (Boerne v. Flores). Following that decision, there were calls in Congress for alternative legislative measures.

Flag Burning

As noted in Chapter 2, this issue ultimately led to attempts to amend the Constitution. In this part, we will discuss the steps from the state law, the Court opinion on that, the federal law, and the Court opinion on that which led up to the amendment efforts.

Continuing Dialogue between the Court and Congress
Court: **Texas v. Johnson** 1989

Congress: Flag Protection Act 1989

Court: **U.S. v. Eichman** 1990

Congress: Amendment attempts 1990, 1995, ? ? ?

Court: In **Texas v. Johnson** (1989), argued March 21, 1989 with the opinion issued June 21, 1989, the Court held (5-4) that the conviction, under a state law, of a political protester who burned an American flag violated the free speech provisions of the First Amendment. Justice Brennan wrote the majority (5-4) opinion. The opinions illustrate many of the points made in Chapter 1 regarding Court opinions.

In the first paragraph of his opinion, Justice Brennan frames the issue:

> After publicly burning an American flag as a means of political protest, Gregory Lee Johnson was convicted of desecrating a flag in violation of Texas law. This case presents the question whether his conviction is consistent with the First Amendment. We hold that it is not.

By framing the issue in terms of political protest, Justice Brennan sets up a greater First Amendment protection for Johnson since political speech is always given greater protection and leeway in our society. Recall the language in **Barnette**, a case Justice Brennan cites often in his opinion.

Justice Brennan notes:

> . . . a principal "function of free speech under our system of government is to invite dispute. It may indeed best serve its high purpose when it induces a condition of unrest, creates dissatisfaction with conditions as they are, or even stirs people to anger."

He goes on to note:

> If there is a bedrock principle underlying the First Amendment, it is that the Government may not prohibit the expression of an idea simply because society finds the idea itself offensive or disagreeable.

Later, citing **Barnette**, he notes:

> If there is any fixed star in our constitutional constellation, it is that no offical high or petty, can prescribe what shall be orthodox in politics, nationalism, religion or other matters of opinion or force citizens to confess by word or act their faith therein.

Justice Brennan was not unaware of the emotional aspects of this case and the opinion of the Court. He addresses that at the end of his opinion.

> Our decision is a reaffirmation of the principles of freedom and inclusiveness that the flag best reflects, and the conviction that our toleration of criticism such as Johnson's is a sign and source of our strength. . . .
>
> The way to preserve the flag's special role is not to punish those who feel differently about these matters. It is to persuade them that they are wrong. . . .
>
> We can imagine no more appropriate response to burning a flag than waving one's own.

In a concurring opinion, Justice Kennedy also displays an awareness of the emotional ramifications of the case. Some of his opinion is set forth in Chapter 2. It bears repeating.

> I write not to qualify the words Justice Brennan chooses so well, for he says with power all that is necessary to explain our ruling. I join his opinion without reservation, but with a keen sense that this case, like others before us from time to time, exacts its personal toll. This prompts me to add to our pages these few remarks.

He goes on to say:

> The hard fact is that sometimes we must make decisions we do not like. We make them because they are right, right in the sense that the law and the Constitution, as we see them, compel the result. And so great is our commitment to the process that, except in the rare case, we do not pause to express distaste for the result, perhaps for fear of undermining a valued principle that dictates the decision. This is one of those rare cases.
>
> . . . the flag is constant in expressing beliefs Americans share, beliefs in law and peace and that freedom which sustains the human spirit. The case here today forces recognition of the costs to which those beliefs commit us. It is poignant but fundamental that the flag protects those who hold it in contempt. . . .
>
> . . . the fact remains that his acts were speech, in both the technical and the fundamental meaning of the Constitution. So I agree with the Court that he must go free.

Congress: Congress passed the Flag Protection Act of 1989 (FPA) in the Fall of 1989. (18 USC 700 10/28/89)

The law provided in part:

> (a) (1) Whoever knowingly mutilates, defaces, physically defiles, burns, maintains on the floor or ground, or tramples upon any flag of the United States shall be fined under this title or imprisoned for not more than one year, or both.

Note: President Bush didn't sign the bill, but did not veto it. There were sufficient votes in Congress for it to become law without his signature. It has been suggested that he'd been advised that it was unconstitutional. The administration did defend the law in the Supreme Court.

Court: In **U.S. v. Eichman** (1990), argued May 14, 1990 with the opinion issued June 11, 1990, the Court held the FPA to be unconstitutional. Justice Brennan again delivered the opinion of the Court, which had the same 5-4 majority alignment. He notes:

> After our decision in Johnson, Congress passed the Flag Protection Act of 1989.

He cites the law and sets forth the relevant part in the body of the opinion. He then notes:

The Government concedes in these cases, as it must, that appellee's flag burning constituted expressive conduct . . . but invites us to reconsider our rejection in Johnson of the claim that flag burning as mode of expression, like obscenity or 'fighting words,' does not enjoy the full protection of the First Amendment. . . . This we decline to do.

He again acknowledges that this will be a difficult opinion.

We are aware that desecration of the flag is deeply offensive to many.

He goes on to cite Johnson regarding bedrock principles underlying the First Amendment.

The overall opinion was shorter than **Johnson**. Justice Kennedy did not write a separate concurrence and the dissents were also shorter.

It is interesting that the Justice who may be considered the most "conservative," Justice Scalia, voted with the majority in both cases, while the justice who may be considered the most "liberal," Justice Stevens, dissented in both cases. It seems a fairly clear illustration of the difficulty of these issues.

Congress: As noted in Chapter 2, after **Eichman**, the amendment efforts started. To date, they have failed. It is doubtful the issue has gone away and in an election year (1996) the issue is sure to come up.

Note: These are ongoing issues and every term the Court seems to address some aspect of them. Between the completion and publication of this book, there may well be further cases and legislative activity on these exact issues.

CONGRESS LEGISLATES TO SOLIDIFY, ENHANCE, OR EXPAND A SUPREME COURT DECISION

This is another area where there is often a continuing dialogue between the Court and Congress. This can occur when the Court considers the constitutionality of some action by a state. The Court will render an opinion and then Congress may follow up with legislation to solidify the opinion of the Court under federal law, or to expand upon the right of action. This action then provides both a written legislative history and codified support if the issue arises in the future.

Since the opinions of the Court are often fact specific, that is, they address only the specific facts and parties before them, there may also remain some uncertainty regarding the applicability of the decision to other somewhat similar situations. For that reason, the Congress may also act to clarify and/or expand the decision. The fact-specific nature of a Court decision may also lead to further lawsuits, since individuals may feel the previous decision does not directly apply to or control their particular factual situation.

This sort of supplemental legislation, often followed by further Court opinions, sometimes results from a lack of detail and/or clarity on the part of Congress and/or the Court. Part of this may be by design; it is difficult to address every possible action and permutation which could arise.

An example of this dialogue (more polite than that previously discussed where Congress and the Court are in disagreement), is found in the following situation regarding use of school facilities by religious groups.

The Court: **Widmar v. Vincent** (1981)

Congress: The Equal Access Act 20 USC 4071-4074 (8/11/84)

The Court: **Board of Education of the Westside Community Schools v. Mergens** (1990)

Court: In **Widmar v. Vincent** (1981), a state university made its facilities generally available for activities of registered student groups. A religious group was denied such use. The Court held 8-1 that the exclusionary policy was unacceptable. Since the university had created a forum generally open to student groups, it could not exclude the religious groups.

Justice Powell stated:

> Through its policy of accommodating their meetings, the University has created a forum generally open for use by student groups. Having done so, the University has assumed an obligation to justify its discriminations and exclusions under applicable constitutional norms. The Constitution forbids a State to enforce certain exclusions from a forum generally open to the public, even if it was not required to create the forum in the first place.
>
> In order to justify discriminatory exclusion from a public forum based on the religious content of a group's intended speech, the University must therefore satisfy the standard of review appropriate to content based exclusions. It must show that its regulation is necessary to serve a compelling state interest and that it is narrowly drawn to achieve that end.

The Court found no such interest in this case and therefore held that access could not be denied. They also held that such equal access would not violate the Establishment Clause since there was no endorsement of any religion and the primary effect of the open forum would not be to advance religion. The Court noted that they would not hold that "an 'equal access' policy would be incompatible with the Court's Establishment clause cases."

Congress: In 1984, Congress enacted The Equal Access Act which provides equal access in any public secondary school. The Act specifically provides as follows:

> It shall be unlawful for any public secondary school which receives Federal financial assistance and which has a limited open forum to deny equal access or a fair opportunity to, or discriminate against, any students who wish to conduct a meet-

ing within that limited open forum on the basis of the religious, political, philosophical, or other content of the speech at such meetings.

The legislation contains definitions of various terms, but does not define specifically all possible terms. Congress may have felt they were defined by implication. Note also that the Act does not address universities. Perhaps Congress felt the law regarding universities was settled by **Widmar**.

Court: In **Westside v. Mergens** (1990), the Court addressed the issue of a public secondary school denying access to a religious group.

Justice O'Connor, in an involved and multipart opinion (recall Chapter 1) states:

> This case requires us to decide whether the Equal Access Act . . . prohibits Westside High School from denying a student religious group permission to meet on school premises during noninstructional time, and, if so, whether the Act, so construed, violates the Establishment Clause of the First Amendment.
>
> Respondents. . . alleged that petitioner's refusal to permit the proposed club to meet at Westside violated the Equal Access Act, 20 USC sections 4071-4074, which prohibits public secondary schools that receive federal financial assistance and that maintain a "limited open forum" from denying "equal access" to students who wish to meet within the forum on the basis of the content of the speech at such meetings. . . Petitioners responded that the Equal Access Act did not apply to Westside and that, if the Act did apply, it violated the Establishment Clause of the First Amendment and was therefore unconstitutional.
>
> . . . In Widmar v. Vincent, supra, we invalidated, on free speech grounds, a state university regulation that prohibited student use of school facilities "for purposes of religious worship or religious teaching." . . . In doing so, we held that an "equal access" policy would not violate the Establishment Clause under our decisions in Lemon v. Kurtzman.

In 1984, Congress extended the reasoning of Widmar to public secondary schools. Under The Equal Access Act, a public secondary school with a "limited open forum" is prohibited from discriminating against students who wish to conduct a meeting within that forum on the basis of the "religious, political, philosophical, or other content of the speech at such meetings."

Justice O'Connor goes on to set forth the precise language of the act and to address some definitional issues. She then continues:

> Unfortunately, the Act does not define the crucial phrase "noncurriculum related student group." Our immediate task is therefore one of statutory interpretation. We begin, of course, with the language of the statute.

After considerable discussion, Justice O'Connor notes:

> . . . we think that the term "noncurriculum related student group" is best interpreted broadly. . . .

The Court held that the group at issue was denied equal access under The Equal Access Act and that the act did not violate the Establishment Clause.

This series of events, case/legislation/case, illustrates the manner in which the Court and Congress work together to resolve an issue about which they seem to agree. It also illustrates the difficulty of legislating for every possible aspect and ramification of complex social issues. In this situation, we again see the tension between the First Amendment dictates prohibiting "establishment" of religion while at the same time protecting the "free exercise" of religion.

CONGRESS DECLINING TO ACT

There may be situations where Congress isn't sure how to proceed or, due to political considerations, feels unable to proceed in a certain manner. These will include instances when legislation was enacted without great detail (Congress couldn't or wouldn't include the detail) and it is left for the Court (or an administrative agency—see below) to interpret the law and "fill in the gaps."

These situations can also include, to a somewhat lesser extent, a dialogue between the Court and Congress. The Congress may set up a situation, by leaving terms open, where the Court has to respond. Sometimes, as we saw in earlier chapters, Congress will then follow up with more legislation.

Vague Terms

Congress: Congress enacted the Civil Rights Act of 1964, with Title VII dealing with discrimination in employment. As noted earlier, "sex" was added at the last minute so there is little legislative history of the intent of Congress regarding sex discrimination in employment. One aspect of sex discrimination in employment which needed to be addressed was that of "sexual harassment."

Often, with this sort of nonspecific legislation, an administrative agency is left with the initial task of "filling in the gaps." In this particular area, the Equal Employment Opportunity Commission (EEOC), has jurisdiction and did issue guidelines in 1980. The guidelines are not binding law, but do provide guidance to parties and the courts.

Court: In **Meritor Savings Bank v. Vinson** (1986), the Court considered the issue of sexual harassment and the CRA of 1964. In a unanimous opinion written by Justice Rehnquist, the Court stated:

> Title VII of the Civil Rights Act of 1964 makes it "an unlawful employment practice for an employer . . . to discriminate against any individual with respect to his compensation, terms, conditions, or privileges of employment, because of such individual's race, color, religion, sex, or national origin." The prohibition against discrimination based on sex was added to Title VII at the last minute on the floor of the House of Representatives.

The Court goes on to note the EEOC guidelines regarding the meaning of "sexual harassment."

> . . . in 1980 the EEOC issued Guidelines specifying that "sexual harassment," as there defined, is a form of sex discrimination prohibited by Title VII.
>
> Since the Guidelines were issued, courts have uniformly held, and we agree, that a plaintiff may establish a violation of Title VII by proving that discrimination based on sex has created a hostile or abusive work environment.

The Court held that a claim of "hostile environment" sex discrimination is actionable under Title VII. They did not specifically define the terms "sexual harassment" or "hostile environment."

Congress: The issue of sexual harassment remained a problem in the workplace. With the confirmation hearings of Clarence Thomas in the fall of 1991, the issue was dramatically in the public eye. Problems existed for both Congress and the Court regarding precise definitions of terms.

In the fall of 1991, Congress enacted the Civil Rights Act of 1991. One of the findings of Congress was:

> . . . additional remedies under Federal law are needed to deter unlawful harassment and intentional discrimination in the workplace. . . .

The act provides additional monetary damages for a complaining party. In this manner, Congress, while being unable to specifically define "sexual harassment," hoped to deter conduct which could be seen as harassment.

Court: In **Harris v. Forklift Systems, Inc.** (1993), the Court again considered the issue of "sexual harassment." A unanimous Court, with Justice O'Connor delivering the opinion, wrestled with the issue of definitions.

> In this case we consider the definition of a discriminatorily "abusive work environment" (also known as a "hostile work environment") under Title VII of the Civil Rights Act of 1964. . . .
>
> This is not, and by its nature cannot be, a mathematically precise test.

The Court was unable to offer a precise definition, but instead listed various factors to consider.

> These may include the frequency of the discriminatory conduct; its severity; whether it is physically threatening or humiliating; or a mere offensive utterance; and whether it unreasonably interferes with an employee's work performance. The effect on the employee's psychological well-being is, of course, relevant to determining whether the plaintiff actually found the environment abusive. But while psychological harm, like any other relevant factor, may be taken into account, no single factor is required.

This situation of defining certain types of conduct and its impact illustrates how the Congress and the Court decline to be precise, while attempting to provide general guidelines. This lack of precise detail can be frustrating for Congress, the Court, and society. Justice Scalia, who is very much in favor of clear, hard-and-fast guidelines, concluded his concurring opinion in Harris as follows:

> I know of no test more faithful to the inherently vague statutory language than the one the Court today adopts.

It appears that in a complex world, exact, precise guidelines may be difficult to attain. This often leaves it up to the states and society to fill in the gaps, as we will discuss in Chapter 4.

Terms Left Out

Sometimes Congress may decline to include terms or provisions in legislation. This may be due to oversight or to political considerations. It may be believed that if certain terms are present the entire legislation may fail. (Recall the issue of adding "sex" to the CRA of 1964 in an attempt to bring about its defeat.)

As noted above, the Civil Rights Act of 1991 created certain rights to recover damages and to have a jury trial in certain actions brought pursuant to federal civil rights laws. The act was in response to certain decisions of the Court. After the act was passed, the Court had to consider an issue not addressed in the legislation.

In **Landgraf v. U.S. Film Products** (1994), the Court had to consider whether the provisions of the act were retroactive. Noting that there is a general presumption against retroactivity, the Court found no intent of Congress that the act be retroactive. Congress had not acted on that matter.

Justice Stevens stated:

> The Civil Rights Act of 1991 is in large part a response to a series of decisions of this Court interpreting the Civil Rights Acts of 1866 and 1964. . . .
>   Other sections of the Act were obviously drafted with "recent decisions of the Supreme Court in mind."

The Court felt that Congress, by failing to act on the matter of retroactivity had essentially acted against it. (It has been suggested that the reason Congress did not act on retroactivity is that had there been such a provision in the act, the act itself might not have passed.) In fact, the previous year, similar civil rights legislation had been vetoed.

After **Landgraf,** there was some discussion in Congress to go back and amend the law again to provide for retroactivity. As of this date, no legislation has been enacted.

There are other times and circumstances when Congress does not act. It may be that political realities make it impossible in some situations. At other times, it is the nature of the legislative process. Congress cannot answer every possible eventuality in legislation. The legislation must be broad enough to encompass a variety of situations. This allows for the freedom of the people to comply with the law while providing some flexibility. If the law is too tight, it will either be too limited or people will find a way around it. The catch is that if it's too loose, the law won't provide sufficient guidelines for conduct. Most legislation falls in the middle somewhere, often leaving the Court in the position of filling in some gaps.

Thus, the Court may fill in these gaps. Sometimes, as we learned, Congress will enact other legislation to counter the Court, and other times Congress may enact legislation to expand the decision of the Court. Or, Congress may do nothing and let matters stand, which means, to a large extent, leave it up to states and society—which we address in Chapter 4.

The States and Society

Who does have final say? Where does this dialogue between the Court and Congress leave us? We have seen how state laws and actions may lead to the dialogue. We have noted there is some "front end" influence of society on the opinions of the Court since the Court is not totally immune to public attitudes. Society also influences legislators in how they carry out their duties. Let's briefly examine the role of the states and then consider various responses of society to some of these difficult and emotional issues.

ROLE OF THE STATES

THE CONSTITUTION OF THE UNITED STATES

Amendment X

The powers not delegated to the United States by the Constitution, nor prohibited by it to the States, are reserved to the States respectively, or to the people.

The relationship of the Court to the states involves the issue of federalism. Federalism is the concept of dividing power between the federal government and the states. Early concerns existed in this country about too much centralized power. The proper allocation and balance of power is an ongoing question and concern. We saw how the Commerce Clause litigation in the New Deal era wrestled with the issue, finally coming down more on the side of federal power with the **Jones & Laughlin** case. Chief Justice Rehnquist discussed this balance of power in the 1995 **Lopez** case.

We start with first principles. The Constitution creates a Federal Government of enumerated powers. See U.S. Const., Art. I Section 8. As James Madison wrote, "(t)he powers delegated by the proposed Constitution to the federal government are few and defined. Those which are to remain in the State governments are numerous and indefinite." . . . This constitutionally mandated division of authority "was adopted by the Framers to ensure protection of our fundamental liberties." . . . "Just as the separation and independence of the coordinate branches of the Federal Government serves to prevent the accumulation of excessive power in any one branch, a healthy balance of power between the States and the Federal Government will reduce the risk of tyranny and abuse from either front."

As Justice Brandeis stated in his dissent in **New State Ice Co. v. Liebmann** (1932),

There must be power in the States and the Nation to remould, through experimentation, our economic practices and institutions to meet changing social and economic needs. . . . To stay experimentation in things social and economic is a grave responsibility. Denial of the right to experiment may be fraught with serious consequences to the nation. It is one of the happy incidents of the federal system that a single courageous state may, if its citizens chose, serve as a laboratory; and try novel social and economic experiments without risk to the rest of the country.

He went on to say:

This Court has the power to prevent an experiment. We may strike down the statute which embodies it on the ground that, in our opinion, the measure is arbitrary, capricious or unreasonable. We have power to do this, because the due process clause has been held by the Court applicable to matters of substance as well as to matters of procedure. But in the exercise of this high power, we must be ever on our guard, lest we erect our prejudices into legal principles. If we would guide by the light of reason, we must let our minds be bold.

The questions remain today: When should the Court exercise that power? How far can an individual state go? What are the limits of federal authority? What are the limits of experimentation?

Many commentators have suggested the current Supreme Court is more of a "statist" court, meaning it is inclined to leave more latitude to the states. Such an attitude seems to prevail in Congress as well. This is reflected in the desire to shift the operation of many social programs to the states, with the use of "block grants," rather than maintaining federal operation and control. As an illustration of the complexity of this (political) issue, consider that the same Congress seems intent on making "tort" law a federally controlled matter. (Tort law includes personal-injury and product-liability laws. Congress is most concerned with product-liability law and the terms "tort reform" and "product-liability reform" often get used interchangeably.)

This relationship between the Court and the states is similar to that of the Court and Congress in that the states may respond to a Court decision in a variety of ways. In situations where the Court has ruled that a state law is unconstitutional, the state may respond with new legislation which is designed to comply with the guidelines (possibly) set forth by the Court. This further state legislation is a common occurrence due to the immediacy of the issues. Since most people are more directly affected by state and local laws, the issues will more often arise in this context.

States may attempt to restrict certain rights guaranteed by the Constitution and the Court. When they do provide less the case may go back to the Court. This results in a continuing dialogue between the states and the Court, similar to the dialogue discussed in Chapter 3 regarding Congress legislating in response to court decisions. We noted in that chapter that much of the dialogue between the Court and Congress starts with the Court rendering an opinion on a state law.

The states are free to provide more protection for individual rights than is set forth in the U.S. Constitution and often do so either through legislation or in their own state constitutions. We saw that situation mentioned in the **Smith** case where Justice Scalia noted that some states do exempt sacramental use of peyote from their drug laws.

An illustration of this expansion of individual liberty, and the dialogue and political activity it generates, can be seen in the area of obscenity. Obscenity is a form of speech which is not protected under the U.S. Constitution. In 1973, the Supreme Court, in **Miller v. California,** attempted to set forth guidelines and definitions (a "test") regarding obscenity. The Court held that material could be obscene if:

> (a) the average person, applying contemporary community standards, would find that the work, taken as a whole, appeals to the prurient interest; and (b) the work depicts or describes, in a patently offensive way, sexual conduct specifically defined by the applicable state law; and (c) the work, taken as a whole, lacks serious literary, artistic, political, or scientific value.

This "definition/test" has led to many subsequent cases. States have responded in a variety of ways. One state, Oregon, has provided that obscenity is within the category of protected speech. In **State v. Henry** (1987), the Oregon Supreme Court held that the Oregon Constitution protects all forms of speech, including obscenity. There have been efforts in Oregon to amend the state constitution to remove that protection. State ballot measures have addressed the issue, with one specifically stating that the state should use the federal standard regarding obscenity.

There are other considerations which may impact the manner in which these issues are addressed by the states. State constitutions are generally easier to amend than is the U.S. Constitution, and many state judges are subject to the political process and can be voted out of office. Also, it is generally easier, due to the smaller number of votes needed, and certainly less expensive, to get elected to a state office. This provides the potential for more extreme viewpoints in the legislative bodies. These considerations can operate to make the discussion of the emotional issues we have discussed more volatile and also to alter the role and response of the judges.

SOCIETY

Amendment IX

The enumeration in the Constitution, of certain rights, shall not be construed to deny or disparage others retained by the people.

We have briefly noted how the public and existing cultural attitudes may influence the writing of court opinions (recall the flag burning cases). Such social and cultural attitudes will certainly impact on society's acceptance, acquiescence, disregard, or defiance of the Court decisions. Strong emotional issues will not disappear simply because the Court has ruled. The ruling will not change long held beliefs. If there is vigorous enforcement, the ruling of law can change actions and conduct. It would be hoped that as conduct is altered, belief may follow. Attitudes will not change overnight, no matter how short, succinct, and strongly stated a court opinion may be. **Brown v. Board of Education** (1954), was short, unanimous, and clear in its principles. We're still waiting for its full implementation. In fact, cases today are still dealing with issues of implementation and continuing court supervision.

We have seen that the Court understands there may be resistance and opposition to its rulings. In cases such as **Brown** they have acknowledged that resistance such as in the following statement: "But it should go without saying that the vitality of these constitutional principles cannot be allowed to yield simply because of disagreement with them" (Chief Justice Warren). As Justice Frankfurter stated in his concurrence to **Cooper v. Aaron** (1958): "The duty to abstain from resistance to 'the Supreme Law of the land,' U.S. Constitution Article 6 paragraph 2, as declared by the organ of our Government for ascertaining it, does not require immediate approval of it nor does it deny the right of dissent. Criticism need not be stifled. Active obstruction or defiance is barred."

DeToqueville noted in *Democracy in America* that the freedom of belief, and to a great extent, conduct in a democracy makes change difficult. There is no dictatorial force to compel compliance. DeToqueville wrote: "Without Justices of the Supreme Court, the Constitution would be a dead letter. Their power is enormous, but it is the power of public opinion. [The Justices] are all powerful as long as the people respect the law; but they would be impotent against popular neglect or contempt of the law." This is another reason written opinions can serve such a vital role; they can encourage and persuade society to "buy in" to the decision by providing persuasive reasoning.

This raises the issue of the enforceability of court decisions. The Court has no direct enforcement power; their primary power is the power of persuasion. There have been instances where this lack of enforcement power has become an issue.

In **The Cherokee Cases** in the 1830s, involving control over certain Cherokee lands, President Jackson refused to enforce a decision of the Court. A quote often attributed to Jackson, but never officially documented, was: "John Marshall has made his decision, now let him enforce it."

In the 1950s and 1960s (and beyond?), the country saw the "massive resistance" to the desegregation cases. In many instances, the executive branch ordered federal troops into states to enforce the laws.

You may recall that during the Watergate matter the Court, in its 1974 opinion **U.S. v. Nixon**, ordered the president to surrender tapes of White House conversations. A possible constitutional crisis loomed in the event the president had defied the order. He did not.

This issue regarding executive privilege and enforceability of Court decisions could arise regarding President Clinton and certain Whitewater documents, as well as in the lawsuit Paula Jones has filed against the president. A lower federal court recently ruled that her lawsuit could proceed against the president while he is in office. In June 1997, the Supreme Court agreed.

The manner in which society responds to actions of the Court and Congress involves many factors. Chapter 1 briefly mentioned some as they relate to the force and clarity of Court opinions. Any detailed analysis of the response of society is beyond the scope of this book. A few general points and illustrations can be made.

When actions of the Court and Congress touch on matters involving deeply held social attitudes and beliefs, further action may be required either by the courts or other branches of government to implement that action. We have looked at a variety of such matters in this book, including:

Abortion

Religion: Establishment Clause

    Prayer in public schools

    Support, promotion, endorsement, or accommodation

Gender: General issues

    Title IX

    Sexual harassment

Flag burning

Now we will look at some of the responses "We the People" have made to court opinions on these matters. We will not delve deeply into the issues, as each is more than enough for a book. We will briefly consider some of the legal, social, and political responses, as well as some problems with the terminology of each issue, to illustrate the complexity and ongoing consideration required in these matters. Keep in mind that the vague nature of the terminology and court opinions may encourage society to act in a manner beyond that which the law requires. In order to avoid falling below the acceptable line of conduct, society may err on the side of doing more. We will see this illustrated, as well as some of the possible problems which can result, in the discussions that follow.

ABORTION

Legal, Social, and Political Responses/Terminology Problems

The year 1998 marks the 25th anniversay of **Roe v. Wade**. The response to the opinion in 1973 was strong from various church leaders, who were critical of the decision. Some of the immediate response was probably muted due to the fact that Lyndon Johnson died on the day the opinion was announced, thereby deflecting attention.

With an emotionally charged issue such as abortion, individuals will not change their feelings simply because of a ruling by the Court. There has been a variety of state legislation resulting in a series of Court cases. There have been issues raised regarding parental notification, spousal notification, judicial approval for minors, waiting periods, issues of funding, issues of advising regarding abortion in federally funded clinics, etc. This stream of legislation and resulting cases illustrates states taking a Court decision and trying to fit a law around/into it. Part of the problem in this and other similarly difficult and emotional matters is that the Court rulings may provide only rather loose or vague guidelines (language like "undue hardship" and "no unreasonable restrictions"), which leave everyone a bit uncertain as to what the law actually allows and/or forbids.

As of this date, **Roe** has not been overturned, but it has been buffeted by storms of litigation and protest, and the Court has allowed a variety of restrictions, and some would say limitations, on the right to an abortion.

This is an emotional issue involving personal, religious, medical, technological, and political feelings and attitudes. It will not go away and will surely continue to spark dialogue between all interested parties, particularly in an election year. As evidence of the difficulty of this issue, emotionally and otherwise, consider the matter of Norma McCorvey, the "Jane Roe" of **Roe**. She recently announced that she was changing her allegiance in this battle and has become supportive of Operation Rescue, a very active "pro-life" group.

As noted, there have been myriad state cases restricting the basic right to an abortion. Part of the success of these cases may be due to a sense of confidence originally felt by supporters of abortion rights after **Roe**. The feeling may have been, "The Supreme Court has ruled, so that takes care of that." As we have seen over the last twenty-plus years, that theory is not the reality.

There may not be any social issue which has generated more vocal and public protest and demonstration than abortion. This protest and demonstration has taken many forms, and has led to further litigation on some of the related legal issues. The abortion issue has generated litigation concerning such matters as free speech as it relates to protest demonstrations at clinics which provide abortion counseling and/or services as well as the application of federal racketeering laws as they may apply to demonstrations at such clinics. Other issues arising include defamation, invasion of privacy, trespass, civil disobedience, choice-of-evils defense, operating standards for clinics, etc. The Supreme Court has been called upon to rule on several of these matters which, while they do not directly require the Court to consider the continued validity of **Roe**, bring, and keep, the issue of abortion at the forefront.

Vast amounts of money are spent on this issue by both sides. Organizations have been created and grown to take either side of the issue. Groups such as Operation Rescue have grown in size and activism. (It is intriguing to note that, at least regarding publicity, it appears that the major leaders of organizations such as Operation Rescue are all men. Since there are certainly many women who oppose the right to an abortion, this is interesting.)

In dealing with this issue, the Court and society are called upon to consider a variety of terms and their meanings. Terms such as "privacy," "liberty," "compelling state interest," "undue burden," are subject to differing interpretations. Additionally, how the issue is framed in the media may also play a role. Is the procedure a "partial birth" abortion or is it an "intact dilation and evacuation" abortion? This has been an issue in the recent action by Congress to ban certain "late term" abortions. Issues of religious faith, time of conception, and technological reliability also play a role.

The issue of emerging technology impacts this issue. The trimester approach in **Roe** may become (or already is?) obsolete as technological advances are such that determinations of viability and ability to sustain life outside the womb are made. (Issues of technology impact many areas of law. Consider the current issues involving the rights and responsibilities of parties on the Internet.)

Another issue is the development of drugs such as RU-486, the "abortion pill." Clinical tests have started for that drug in the United States. If the drug reaches the market, it creates a somewhat different atmosphere for the issue since obtaining an abortion might not necessarily require going to an "abortion clinic." Some groups, in sensing this, have attempted to apply pressure to prevent making the drug available.

"Public Opinion" Polls

Everybody has a poll on this issue. All polls should be taken with a grain, or a pound, of salt. The context of the poll; the group polled; the timing, content, nature, and order of the questions are all variables to be considered. How the responses are interpreted and reported can also be open to question. These factors are equally applicable to all polls involving volatile social issues.

Abortion Rights Polls: Some of the various questions asked in polls are the following:

> Would you vote for a candidate who is "pro-life?"
>
> Would you vote for a candidate who is "pro-choice?"
>
> Do you agree with Roe? (Consider the length, nature of the opinion)
>
> Should federal tax dollars be used for abortions?
>
> Should federally funded clinics give advice regarding abortion?
>
> Should victims of rape be entitled to an abortion?
>
> Should victims of incest be entitled to an abortion?
>
> Should abortion be used where severe birth defects are present?
>
> Should abortion be used as a means of selecting sex of the child?
>
> Should there be a waiting period?
>
> Should parents of minors be notified?
>
> Should the husband be notified?
>
> Should the father be notified?
>
> Should the father be able to prevent the abortion?
>
> Should the doctor have a say?

The extent and scope of these few questions illustrates part of the complexity. The polls do seem to be asking clearer questions when compared to the following sort of questions from groups on either extreme of the debate:

1. Do you want your hard earned tax dollars to go to pay for welfare mothers' use of abortion as a convenient form of birth control?
2. To you want to see the law changed so that young, unwed women from abusive, broken homes will have to resort to back alley, life threatening abortions?

The use of polls can be valuable. It can also mislead and contribute more to the solidification of existing attitudes and opinions rather than to a resolution or to intelligent debate.

Has the Response of Society Made the Law?

Consider that the issue has become some sort of a "litmus test" for political candidates and nominees for the Supreme Court. Recall how many felt Clarence Thomas might have been somewhat disingenuous when he said he had never debated **Roe v. Wade** when asked during his confirmation hearings what his feelings were toward that case. Consider that the issue relates to political candidates and political parties, particularly during an election year. Candidates who may feel moderate on the issue, may wind up getting heat from both sides. Sometimes, politicians may find themselves voting for legislation which they feel may not pass the Court's constitutional checkpoint, but which makes them feel good, and look good to some constituents. Certainly, the continuing protests and reframing of the question has contributed to uncertainty and constant evaluation, reevaluation, and reconsideration of the issues in public and private forums.

RELIGION: ESTABLISHMENT CLAUSE

Legal, Social, and Political Responses/Terminology Problems: Prayer in Public Schools

Most polls show that a majority of society favors prayer in schools. Various politicians favor it. In many schools, prayer continues despite the rulings of the Court which hold that mandated prayer in schools violates the Establishment Clause of the First Amendment. It is often left to private individuals to file lawsuits in order to compel compliance with the Court decisions.

The Court's decision in **Engel**, in 1962, set off an immediate response. Church leaders criticized the ruling and there were over one hundred proposals for action in Congress. As we saw in Chapter 2, the Court has consistently held that government-mandated prayer in public schools is not allowed under the Constitution.

At the time of **Engel**, 1962, society was in a period of unrest and social protest. It was the era of the counterculture and questioning of authority, including traditional religions. Recent years have seen a revival of religion and the rise politically of such groups as the Christian Coalition. This revival and publicity has provided political groups with their "litmus tests," similar to that of certain groups in the abortion debate. Other parties contend that mandating some form of generic prayer in the schools actually operates to trivialize religion because of the generic nature of such "prayer" and the compulsory manner of its recitation.

Part of the impetus for these groups has been the lack of clarity in the Court opinions and their meaning. We will see in other areas how the uncertainty of the law can possibly work for the betterment of society, when individuals and/or organizations go beyond the moral minimums of the law's requirements. This can be seen regarding the issue of sexual harassment discussed later in the chapter. However, it can also work to provide misleading examples of the law's intent and operation—and perhaps create a backlash. For instance, some school officials, for fear of violating the law, have reacted beyond what may have been intended and created opportunities for groups to speak of the law's hostility towards religion. There have been cases where a teacher has prohibited a student from even reading the Bible at school.

The courts, including the Supreme Court, have seen numerous cases regarding the issue of prayer and schools. Part of this stream of cases is the result of defiance of the Court, partly due to attempts to work around the incremental, fact specific Court opinions, and partly due to local majorities disagreeing with the Court and continuing with prayer until challenged. This may occur if the majority of the local community and/or school board is in favor of prayer in the public schools. In some areas, the prayer goes on, and nobody complains. When a complaint is made and the matter goes to court, the Court will hold the prayer is a violation of the Constitution. This sort of private enforcement can be seen below regarding Title IX, gender equity, when the plaintiffs (women who are denied equity) bring suit and win. Without private efforts at enforcement, the opinion of the Court and/or the statutory law will continue to be violated.

Another reason for the stream of cases relates to the terminology involved and the problems with coming to any agreed upon definitions. Trying to reach an agreed upon meaning for terms such as "entanglement," "endorsement," and "accommodation" is difficult. Given the complex and prevailing nature of the federal governments' involvement in our lives, the matter of "entanglement" becomes increasingly problematical. This does not even begin to address the differing opinions on matters such as "values," "family values," "Judeo-Christian values," "Christian values," and more.

This issue will not go away, although it has abated a bit at this time. This may be in part due to a statement issued by President Clinton in which he basically set forth what is allowed in public schools under existing Court rulings. Far from "taking God out of the classroom," there is a great deal of leeway regarding religion in the schools. A large part of the problem seems to be activist parties on both sides, those who feel there should be mandatory teacher-led prayers and those who feel there should be no prayer at all. There is a continuing climate of such uncertainty that administrators in the schools have no clear guidelines for their actions.

"Public Opinion" Polls

There are lots of polls on this issue. Again, the nature, content, and extent of the questions can be illustrative:

Do you favor prayer in school?

Should prayer be permitted in schools?

Should religion be studied in school?

Should religious study be compelled?

Should prayer be compulsory?

Should state mandated and drafted prayer be mandated?

Should students be prevented from reading the Bible in school?

Should students be allowed to pray in class?

Should students be allowed to pray on their own time?

Where? When? How? With teachers?

Has the Response of Society Made the Law?

Certainly this issue is alive and subject to debate, which indicates the emotion and complexity involved. The political aspects raised by such groups as the Christian Coalition. Their power of endorsement for certain political candidates illustrates that society can impact the law in this area. The local activity and power of school boards, which may include a majority wanting prayer in the schools, illustrates the ongoing tension of the issue and the likelihood of a continuing series of court cases at the lower level as well as in the Supreme Court.

Support, Promotion, Endorsement, or Accommodation

Much like the abortion issue, there have been many instances where the Court has been called upon to evaluate state laws under the "Lemon Test." These have included laws regarding nonfinancial aid to religious schools, such as bus services (permitted), textbooks (permitted), as well as tax deductions for educational costs (permitted). The Court, in keeping with Justice Burger's opinion, has addressed these on a case-by-case basis.

Another area where establishment clause issues arise is that of public displays of religious symbols. This seems to arise around Christmas each year when some city or other governmental body chooses to display some sort of religious symbol. The issue is whether such displays establish religion. The Court wrestles with this issue in the case-by-case look at all the facts and circumstances manner that was set forth in **Lemon**. The opinions tend to be long, detailed, and fragmented. The key fact in these cases seems to be whether it appears that the government itself is "endorsing" any particular religion over others. If that is the case, the symbols must go.

In 1995, the Court revisited this issue in **Capitol Square Review Board v. Pinette**. Justice Scalia stated:

> The question in this case is whether a State violates the Establishment Clause when, pursuant to a religiously neutral state policy, it permits a private party to display an unattended religious symbol in a traditional public forum located next to its seat of government.

The Court held that it did not. Justice Scalia was able to distinguish the case from those in which a governmental body had placed some sort of religious display. While Justice O'Connor concurred in the judgment, she chose to further address the issue of endorsement of religion.

> In recent years, we have paid particularly close attention (in Establishment Clause cases) to whether the challenged governmental practice either has the purpose or effect of "endorsing" religion, a concern that has long had a place in our Establishment Clause jurisprudence. . . . A government statement "that religion or a particular religious belief is favored or preferred," . . . violates the prohibition against establishment of religion because such (e)ndorsement sends a message to nonadherents that they are outsiders, not full members of the political community, and an accompanying message to adherents that they are insiders, favored members of the political community.

She goes on to note:

> In the end, I would recognize that the Establishment Clause inquiry cannot be distilled into a fixed, per se rule. [Author's note: A "per se" rule means that if certain facts could be established, the Court would know exactly how to rule without further inquiry. Recall Chapter 1 regarding Court Opinions.] Thus, (e)very government practice must be judged in its unique circumstances to determine whether it constitutes an endorsement or disapproval of religion.

This case illustrates to some degree the different approaches of Justice Scalia and Justice O'Connor. While he is more inclined to set some hard and fast rules, she is more inclined to go case by case, depending on each case's particular facts and circumstances. The **Capitol Square** case presented troubling facts since the display at issue was a cross to be placed by the Ku Klux Klan. Justice Scalia found that the expression was private, and in a public forum which was open to all on equal terms, and therefore did not violate the Establishment Clause. Justice O'Connor found that under the particular facts, the government did not appear to take any position on religious belief or make adherence to any particular belief relevant to a person's standing in the political community, and therefore did not violate the Establishment Clause.

Confusing? Consider how the opinion was announced:

> SCALIA, J., announced the judgment of the Court and delivered the opinion of the Court with respect to Parts I, II, III, in which REHNQUIST, C.J., and O'CONNOR, KENNEDY, SOUTER, THOMAS, and BREYER, JJ., joined, and an opinion with respect to Part IV, in which REHNQUIST, C.J., and KENNEDY and THOMAS, JJ., joined. THOMAS, J., filed a concurring opinion. O'CONNOR, J., filed an opinion concurring in part and concurring in the judgment, in which SOUTER and BREYER, JJ., joined. SOUTER, J., filed an opinion concurring in part and concurring in the judgment, in which O'CONNOR and BREYER, JJ., joined. STEVENS, J., and GINSBURG, J., filed dissenting opinions.

Recall Chapter 1 regarding the Court opinions. In many of these complex areas of the law, this sort of opinion is the norm with the justices so fragmented it is difficult for the rest of us to understand what was said and what it means.

GENDER: GENERAL ISSUES

Legal, Social, and Political Responses/Terminology Problems

The social reality is that there are more women working outside the home and in businesses. As a result, the issues of pregnancy and parental leave take on a greater economic importance. More companies want to provide some form of parental leave to their employees rather than risk losing good and valuable employee resources. Many states have enacted some form of parental leave into their laws. Note that *now* this sort of leave is gender neutral and applies to both parents. Originally, it was a "maternal" leave. Men felt this was gender discrimination. Congress enacted the Family Leave Act as a follow-up to this issue.

Since the cases in the 1970s such as **Frontiero** (1973), there has been a greater awareness of the issue of gender and equality of treatment. Certainly the Equal Rights Amendment contributed to the discussion and debate. Since the seventies, many issues related to equality of treatment among the sexes have come to our attention—issues involving the "glass ceiling," membership in "private" clubs, opportunities in certain jobs, the military, women in combat, etc. Existing cultural biases and stereotypes have been challenged. In a case in 1978 involving different pension contributions based upon gender, **Los Angeles v. Manhart**, Justice Stevens stated:

> Even a true generalization about a class is an insufficient reason for disqualifying an individual to whom the generalization does not apply.

Think about how many women are in certain types of jobs, e.g., congresspersons, governorships, high government officials, CEOs, judgeships. There are currently two women on the Supreme Court. Consider the problems they encountered in getting jobs after law school. Sandra Day O'Connor was apparently only offered a job as a secretary. Ruth Bader Ginsburg was unable to find a job in New York City. Would outstanding female law graduates have that same problem today? Some studies suggest that even now that may be so.

The growing role of women in the economy has created awareness as well as problems. Some people are not "comfortable" with women in certain jobs or levels of authority. There has also been a form of backlash among some segments of society, including some female writers and commentators. This has lead to articles about feminism being dead and so forth.

Many interesting cases continue through the courts concerning issues of gender. In a recent case in Florida, the Florida Supreme Court tossed out a 100-year-old law that made husbands responsible for their wives' necessaries, such as food, clothing, and shelter. The law had been created at a time, 1895, when women were unable to own property or enter into contracts. In many of the cases, terminology is an issue. Recall the standard of scrutiny we discussed in Chapter 3 and the question of "compelling" or "important" interests.

"Public Opinion" Polls

Many of the polls in this area tend to be on a specific issue of gender, such as abortion or sexual harassment. Rather than polls, there tend to be "studies" of the issue of gender and possible gender discrimination. Questions tend to be:

Do you expect to be in the work force at age 35?

What is your major field of study?

Do you plan to get a graduate degree?

Do you plan to keep working after childbirth?

The studies consider the percentages of women in the business world, in certain fields, and tend to show the numbers as growing. These numbers can provide an incentive for others to follow. However, the studies also show women still earn less than men, are more likely to hold certain, lower level, types of jobs, have encountered some form of discrimination, and have far less representation at the upper levels of management.

Has the Response of Society Made the Law?

Consider some of the changes which have occurred or are occurring regarding the role/issue of gender in our society.

Formerly "private" clubs are admitting women. In part this is due to a legal challenge as to the nature of the club, with the issue of whether it is private or not, often being resolved in favor of those who say it's not really a private club. However, many private clubs are opening their doors in order to preempt legal action. These include many private golf clubs and some "fraternal" organizations such as the Elks.

Consider other ways in which the roles/perceptions of women and girls may have changed. Girls play Little League baseball. Women in the clergy are not uncommon. Women are, sometimes, portrayed differently in advertisements, on television, and in the movies. (Sometimes they are portrayed in the "traditional" manner.) Women attend the service academies. State-supported public schools may not be able to exclude women. The Court recently heard a case involving Virginia Military Institute (VMI), in which that precise issue was raised. In June 1996, the Court held VMI's categorical exclusion of women was a violation of equal protection under the Constitution, and women entered VMI in August, 1997.

Employers are making changes in their treatment of women employees for economic reasons, as well as to stay ahead of the courts. Many provide day-care, flex-time, job sharing, and other programs to accommodate and retain valued employees.

The first "Take Your Daughter to Work" day was introduced in 1993. It is indicative of the backlash that there were complaints about boys being excluded. Recall how many of the gender equality cases arose from the complaints of men.

Now we will look at a couple of specific gender issues—Title IX and sexual harassment.

TITLE IX

Legal, Social, and Political Responses/Terminology Problems

This law is still violated, in large part due to the attitudes of those in power. It is not unlike racial discrimination. It is often a case of the "haves" not wanting to relinquish anything to the "have nots." The same phrases and rationalizations are used. Since athletics, and especially football, is impacted, there are strong cultural issues involved. As we have noted, the Court (or Congress) can't change attitudes, but they may be able to change conduct. (See Justice Frankfurter's language in **Cooper v. Aaron** (1958) regarding the difference between disagreement and defiance.)

The issue of gender equity involves much of the same cultural baggage of traditional sex discrimination. However, since sport, and often football, is a focal point, the tension is heightened. Many people assume that to provide equal opportunity for women means that football will be destroyed and that football provides all the money for all other sports. The reality is quite different. While football brings in great amounts of money, it also spends great (in many instances, greater) amounts. In most programs, cuts in the football program would have no impact on competitiveness. Consider that NCAA Division I schools have 85 scholarships for football. That is nearly twice the size of professional teams.

This is an area where there has been little public enforcement. There has been much more private enforcement. Many lawsuits have been filed in this area. Consistently, the schools lose. People don't seem to get it. It illustrates problems with the law in general. There is a large private cost to bring litigation. There is no enforcement mechanism. The Court has to rely on the executive branch, states, and society.

Recall that **Franklin v. Gwinnett** came 20 years after the enactment of Title IX, which was designed to provide "gender equity" in educational institutions receiving federal funds. The issue of gender equity in education has met with constant resistance. The **Franklin** case, by providing monetary damages for those denied equitable treatment, may have provided an incentive for those discriminated against to speak up and, if necessary, sue. Often, the possibility of large damages and/or penalties for violation of the law will provide the necessary incentive for greater voluntary compliance.

The **Franklin** case involved sexual harassment and not the more common issue of equitable support for athletics. The holding in **Franklin** of the availability of damage awards did seem to influence that issue. Since **Franklin**, there has been a nearly constant stream of cases brought by women feeling they have been discriminated against, generally in athletics, and that Title IX has been violated. They have consistently won in the lower courts. As these cases get reported, awareness of the law grows as well as awareness of the impact of violating the law. Such information provides a sense of confidence for others to speak out, as well as an incentive for educational institutions to comply with the law in order to avoid damaging lawsuits.

"Public Opinion" Polls

This is another area where the framing of the questions, the order of the questions, etc., can have an impact.

Do you favor equity in funding schools?

Do you favor gutting men's sports just for the sake of seeing whether women want to play or not?

Do you want your daughter to be treated equally?

Do you want to ruin football?

Has the Response of Society Made the Law?

Certainly the trend of women bringing suit and winning is having some influence. As awareness grows and as the Supreme Court seems to endorse the concept, confidence to speak up grows.

Certain opinion makers are also speaking up in favor of the goals of Title IX. *Sports Illustrated* (home of the "Swimsuit Issue") and other traditional sports publications have run articles and editorials on the issue, in addition to those found in "women's" publications or legal publications. Law review articles are written about Title IX and the related legal ramifications.

The NCAA and many schools are starting to provide some education on the issue of Title IX. These educational programs are designed to clear up some of the uncertainties regarding the law, its intent, and requirements. The goal, as in other areas of law, is that if people understand the law, and not just apocryphal stories about it, people will be more likely to comply. Recall again that the law is just a moral minimum.

There are many more women and girls active and participating in sports than prior to Title IX. The increased awareness generated by court cases has only furthered that expansion. Consider the media coverage of women's sports in the last few years. At some schools, the women's basketball teams outdraw the men's. There is a National Girls and Women in Sports Day. You may have seen a recent Nike advertisement on television, where there are lots of little girls saying, "If you let me play . . ." followed by such comments as

> I will be less likely to become pregnant before I want to.
>
> I will be more likely to stay in school.
>
> I will be less likely to let a man abuse me.

Consider where we are as a society and how we have responded to statutory law and the Supreme Court. Nobody is supposed to be in a position to have the power to "let" the little girls play. It is their right. It is indicative of the social realities and hurdles that it requires further court action to compel those in power to "let" someone exercise their rights. The advertisement does do a nice job of raising and framing the issue.

This issue of "letting" someone exercise a right seems to be a constant in discrimination issues. Often, one factor is the issue of the "haves" versus the "have nots." When legislation or court decisions state that the "haves" may have to relinquish a bit so that those who have traditionally been the "have nots" can attain a fairer share, the "haves" tend to resist. In part, this is simple human nature. There are other factors as well. Often, in these situations, there is a lack of information being made available. What does the law really say? This also relates to the issues of force and clarity of the Court opinions mentioned earlier.

There is some terminology which requires understanding. The lower court case law, as well as the administrative agency guidelines, have established a "test" for Title IX compliance. It is a three pronged test. There must be (1) proportionality of participants, (2) a recent history of program expansion for the underrepresented sex, or (3) the school must fully accommodate the interests and abilities of the underrepresented sex. If a school meets any of the three, they are in compliance. In April 1997, the Supreme Court declined to review a District Court opinion (**Cohen v. Brown**) which endorsed the test and favored the female athletes.

SEXUAL HARASSMENT

Legal, Social, and Political Responses/Terminology Problems

The first time the Supreme Court dealt with the issue of sexual harassment was in the 1986 **Meritor** case. While that case certainly raised some awareness of the issue, the Clarence Thomas-Anita Hill situation which came forward in the Fall of 1991 during the hearings on Thomas' confirmation to the

Supreme Court was probably the key turning point for societal awareness of the issue. The Navy's Tailhook problem arose since then. The Supreme Court ruled in the **Harris** case in the Fall of 1993. The Senator Robert Packwood situation brought the issue center stage once more in 1995.

It seems now as if there is an article in the newspaper (any paper) about a sexual harassment claim nearly every week. (If nothing else, the Paula Jones case has sparked discussion on the issue). It may be that the rulings of the Court and the increased awareness have given courage to those who have been harassed to come forward. We saw in the Packwood situation that many women noted that coming forward years ago would've been fruitless. In any event, the increased awareness seems to feed on itself and lead to more litigation. This is consistent with the issue of Title IX enforcement.

If nothing else, society is well aware of the issue of sexual harassment. It does involve a great deal of cultural baggage regarding the roles of men and women, just as in the situations we've seen above regarding gender and Title IX. Sex is not a topic many of us are comfortable discussing, but the increased publicity has made sexual harassment an issue to be discussed in both private and public life.

In response to this increased awareness, many organizations, companies, schools, etc., are attempting to stay ahead of the law and lawsuits by instituting educational programs as well as implementing policies to address the issue. Again, this is consistent with other areas of law.

Part of the difficulty in this area, as in others, is the meaning applied to the terminology. Recall that in **Harris**, even Justice Scalia admitted an inability to come up with an exact definition of the term. The Court simply listed various factors to consider, including the frequency, the severity, whether it was physically threatening or humiliating and so forth. Many terms were left open for interpretation. What is "sexual harassment?" What is a "hostile" environment? What does it mean to "unreasonably interfere" with work? Where is the line between boorish behavior and actionable sexual harassment? Again, many companies and individuals decide to err on the side of discretion and raise the line.

This uncertainty, and the fact of some raising the line on what is or isn't acceptable or at least tolerable conduct, has created problems. There can be a sort of backlash when every word, look or glance is considered sexual harassment. There is a risk of trivializing the issue if a glance is considered sexual harassment. If a glance is, then the perception may be that sexual harassment is not very serious or harmful, and truly serious cases may be ignored.

"Public Opinion" Polls

There can be problems with polls in this area. Sometimes the "polls" are done in the form of "studies."

Have you ever been sexually harassed?

Do you know someone who has been sexually harassed?

Has anyone in your company ever been a victim of harassment?

Do you know that sexual harassment costs the American economy $25 million a year?

At the core is the perhaps personalized definition of the key term. Is it:

coercion

advances

asking for a date

continuing to ask for a date

comments (such as?) about physical appearance

pinups (where)

favoritism

graffiti (where?)

jokes (where, when?)

Polls/studies have shown that there has been a great increase in the number of sexual-harassment complaints. This may mean sexual harassment is more prevalant, simply reported more, misreported, or subject to a variety of interpretations which could result in more actions being considered, by someone, to be "sexual harassment."

Has the Response of Society Made the Law?

Like other areas where the law is somewhat vague, it may well be left to society to make the law. As we see, many companies and individuals will make the law more stringent than perhaps was intended by either the Court or Congress. One possible result of that is the backlash reaction of those who are found to violate the law. This has occurred when individuals who have been fired for sexual harassment have filed wrongful discharge claims against the company. There are also issues of free speech which have been raised. This simply illustrates the complexity of the issue.

In any event, the nearly constant publicity as various cases are filed keeps the awareness level up, which tends to encourage compliance. Many of the cases which get to court seem very clear on their facts. Despite the noted problems of perception and terminology, it generally isn't difficult to find sexual harassment when a supervisor asks a subordinate to go to the hotel to negotiate their raise, reach down his pants to get some coins, bend over so he can look at her, and so forth. Justice Ginsburg, in her concurring opinion in **Harris**, suggested:

The critical issue . . . is whether members of one sex are exposed to disadvantageous terms or conditions of employment to which members of the other sex are not exposed.

Consider how this "test" might apply to other areas. In Title IX, it has been suggested that a "test" of compliance would be for men and women to simply trade positions regarding the resources being made available to them. If the men are just as happy with what they have after the switch, then the institution is probably in compliance.

FLAG BURNING

The response to the **Texas v. Johnson** and **U.S. v. Eichman** decisions was not a sudden rush to burn flags. The flag generates emotion and there was a large, temporary uproar, which passed. It was recognized that a very small minority of people are going to be inclined to burn a flag. Some flags were burned as an illustration of free speech at law schools, but that's about all. A handful of other flag burnings did occur.

As has been noted by the Court (and others) on numerous occasions, when confronted with speech we do not like, we have choices—meet and combat it with more speech and put our trust in the marketplace of ideas, or ignore it and trust it will go away due to its own lack of substance. To a large extent, this was the response to the few incidents of flag burning. These choices relate to other forms of speech which we may disapprove, including hate speech, obscenity, etc.

In all these areas, it appears that the response of society is one part in the continuing conversation between the Court, Congress, the states, and society regarding the law and its application to our everyday lives. The conversation will continue.

Closing Comments

From the foregoing, can we determine who has the "final say"? It seems more likely, particularly on matters involving social, cultural, and emotionally maintained attitudes and beliefs, that it is a cooperative, ongoing process, discussion, dialogue, and debate. While that may not leave us with a great deal of certainty, it may be the best we can do.

From the Introduction we learned a few basic concepts which guide us. The idea of balancing interests of the parties involved is a key as we all try to draw lines for acceptable conduct. Remember: *the law is not designed to compel the best in us; it is designed to prevent the worst.* Where that precise line is drawn is often difficult to determine. The Court attempts to formulate tests to assist us in that determination. The tests are also an effort to set forth objective standards for our guidance. We have seen such tests as:

The Lemon Test regarding establishment of religion.

The endorsement test regarding establishment of religion.

The Miller Test regarding obscenity.

There are other tests for speech (e.g., the O'Brien Test), and for sexual harassment, where the Court, for example in **Harris**, did not set down a precise test, but rather *factors* to be considered. As Title IX litigation works its way towards the Court, the **Brown** three-pronged test has been set forth to gauge compliance with Title IX. The problem with these tests is that even the purportedly objective criteria are often subject to interpretation and debate. Recall the discussion as to whether terms should be given a *broad* or *narrow* interpretation. Where to draw the line is problematical. Consider:

When does a regulation on the right to an abortion, which satisfies a "compelling governmental interest," become an "undue burden"?

When does "expressive conduct," or "symbolic speech," become a wrongful act?

When does "accommodation" of religion become an "endorsement"?

When does a "facially neutral" law become a "substantial burden" on the free exercise of religion?

When does boorish behavior become "sexual harassment"?

We have seen that members of the Court look at the same facts and disagree on the interpretation. So do members of Congress. So do we. These difficult questions, and the need for ongoing discussion and debate, are not limited to the areas we have mentioned. Consider how these same issues and difficulties arise in matters such as race, affirmative action, employment discrimination, the death penalty, the issue of right to die, and other emotionally charged matters.

Awareness of the issue and recognition of the complexity is vital. Modern society is complex and full of nuance. It defies easy answers. With the current Court tending to be incremental and dealing with the specific facts involved with each particular case, it is likely that these dialogues between the Court, Congress, the states, and society will continue. Since so much is fact specific, it is important for all of us to seek out all the facts of a given situation. While this is sometimes difficult, it is also imperative.

The discussion will continue, and an appreciation of the complexity may enable us to listen to those on the other side of the issue. Through open discussion, perhaps awareness and some semblance of consensus or compromise can be achieved. I recall the example of a male coach at an institution wrestling with Title IX. Great animosity and unrest was present as the school tried to deal with the legal realities. At one point during the debate as to women's participation in sports, the coach, who was not terribly supportive of the goals of Title IX on the campus, took part in an unrelated conversation in which he noted just how much self-confidence and personal growth his daughters had achieved through their participation in youth soccer programs.

There are many points of view, opinions, and deeply felt emotions on these social and legal issues. Amidst the confusion and conflict, I find it helpful to keep in mind an old saying:

If you only know your side of the question, you don't even know that.

Epilogue

It's both fun and frustrating to study and write about the law. While it's fun to observe the process, it can be frustrating to struggle to stay current. During the completion of this book, various cases and issues have arisen which illustrate the continuing dialogue between the Court, Congress, the states, and society. Many of these issues are constantly recurring since they involve interpretation of terms, both constitutional and legislative, and affect emotionally charged aspects of our lives. Be on the lookout for cases, legislation, and conversation regarding these matters, including the following:

1. The power of Congress relative to that of the states.
2. A variety of speech issues, including flag burning, obscenity, demonstrations, etc.
3. Abortion issues, including the basic right, limitations, funding, etc.
4. Religious issues, including school prayer and the line between church and state.
5. Gender issues, including sexual harassment, discrimination in institutions receiving federal funds (Title IX), etc.

APPENDIX A

The Constitution of the United States

THE PREAMBLE

We the People of the United States, in Order to form a more perfect Union, establish Justice, insure domestic Tranquility, provide for the common defense, promote the general Welfare, and secure the Blessings of Liberty to ourselves and our Posterity, do ordain and establish this Constitution for the United States of America.

ARTICLE I—THE LEGISLATIVE ARTICLE

Legislative Power

Section 1 All legislative Powers herein granted shall be vested in a Congress of the United States, which shall consist of a Senate and House of Representatives.

House of Representatives: Composition; Qualifications; Apportionment; Impeachment Power

Section 2 The House of Representatives shall be composed of Members chosen every second Year by the People of the several States, and the Electors in each State shall have the Qualifications requisite for Electors of the most numerous Branch of the State Legislature.

No Person shall be a Representative who shall not have attained to the Age of twenty five Years, and been seven Years a Citizen of the United States, and who shall not, when elected, be an Inhabitant of that State in which he shall be chosen.

Representatives and direct Taxes[1] shall be apportioned among the several

---

[1]Modified by the 16th Amendment

States which may be included within this Union, according to their respective Numbers, *which shall be determined by adding to the whole Number of free Persons, including those bound to Service for a Term of Years, and excluding Indians not taxed, three fifths of all other Persons.*[2] The actual Enumeration shall be made within three Years after the first Meeting of the Congress of the United States, and within every subsequent Term of ten Years, in such Manner as they shall by Law direct. The Number of Representatives shall not exceed one for every thirty Thousand, but each State shall have at least one Representative; and until each enumeration shall be made, the State of New Hampshire shall be entitled to chuse three, Massachusetts eight, Rhode-Island and Providence Plantations one, Connecticut five, New-York six, New Jersey four, Pennsylvania eight, Delaware one, Maryland six, Virginia ten, North Carolina five, South Carolina five, and Georgia three.

When vacancies happen in the Representation from any State, the Executive Authority thereof shall issue Writs of Election to fill such Vacancies.

The House of Representatives shall chuse their Speaker and other Officers; and shall have the sole Power of Impeachment.

Senate Composition: Qualifications, Impeachment Trials

Section 3 The Senate of the United States shall be composed of two Senators from each State, *chosen by the Legislature thereof,*[3] for six Years; and each Senator shall have one Vote.

Immediately after they shall be assembled in Consequence of the first Election, they shall be divided as equally as may be into three Classes. The Seats of the Senators of the first Class shall be vacated at the Expiration of the second Year, of the second Class at the Expiration of the fourth Year, and of the third Class at the Expiration of the sixth Year, so that one third may be chosen every second Year; *and if Vacancies happen by Resignation, or otherwise, during the Recess of the Legislature of any State, the Executive thereof may make temporary Appointments until the next Meeting of the Legislature, which shall then fill such Vacancies.*[4]

No person shall be a Senator who shall not have attained to the Age of thirty Years, and been nine Years a Citizen of the United States, and who shall not, when elected, be an inhabitant of that State for which he shall be chosen.

The Vice President of the United States shall be President of the Senate, but shall have no Vote, unless they be equally divided.

The Senate shall chuse their other Officers, and also a President pro tempore, in the Absence of the Vice President, or when he shall exercise the Office of President of the United States.

The Senate shall have the sole Power to try all Impeachments. When sitting for

---

[2]Replaced by Section 2, 14th Amendment
[3]Repealed by the 17th Amendment
[4]Modified by the 17th Amendment

that Purpose, they shall be on Oath or Affirmation. When the President of the United States is tried, the Chief Justice shall preside: And no Person shall be convicted without the Concurrence of two thirds of the Members present.

Judgment in Cases of Impeachment shall not extend further than to removal from Office, and disqualification to hold and enjoy any Office of honor, Trust or Profit under the United States; but the Party convicted shall nevertheless be liable and subject to Indictment, Trial, Judgment and Punishment, according to law.

Congressional Elections: Times, Places, Manner

Section 4 The Times, Places and Manner of holding Elections for Senators and Representatives, shall be prescribed in each State by the Legislature thereof; but the Congress may at any time by Law make or alter such Regulations, except as to the Places of chusing Senators.

The Congress shall assemble at least once in every Year, *and such Meeting shall be on the first Monday in December, unless they shall by Law appoint a different Day.*[5]

Powers and Duties of the Houses

Section 5 Each House shall be the Judge of the Elections, Returns and Qualifications of its own Members, and a Majority of each shall constitute a Quorum to do Business; but a smaller Number may adjourn from day to day, and may be authorized to compel the Attendance of absent Members, in such Manner, and under the Penalties as each House may provide.

Each House may determine the Rules of its Proceedings, punish its Members for disorderly Behaviour, and, with the Concurrence of two thirds, expel a Member.

Each House shall keep a Journal of its Proceedings, and from time to time publish the same, excepting such Parts as may in their Judgment require Secrecy; and the Yeas and Nays of the Members of either House on any question shall, at the Desire of one fifth of those Present, be entered on the Journal.

Neither House, during the Session of Congress, shall, without the Consent of the other, adjourn for more than three days, nor to any other place than that in which the two Houses shall be sitting.

Rights of Members

Section 6 The Senators and Representatives shall receive a Compensation for their Services, to be ascertained by Law, and paid out of the Treasury of the United States. They shall in all Cases, except Treason, Felony and Breach of the Peace, be privileged from Arrest during their Attendance at the Session of their respective Houses, and in going to and returning from the same; and for any Speech or Debate in either House, they shall not be questioned in any other Place.

---

[5]Changed by the 20th Amendment

No Senator or Representative, shall, during the time for which he was elected, be appointed to any civil Office under the Authority of the United States, which shall have been created, or the Emoluments whereof shall have been encreased during such time; and no Person holding any Office under the United States, shall be a Member of either House during his Continuance in Office.

Legislative Powers: Bills and Resolutions

Section 7 All Bills for raising Revenue shall originate in the House of Representatives; but the Senate may propose or concur with Amendments as on other Bills.

Every Bill which shall have passed the House of Representatives and the Senate, shall, before it becomes a Law, be presented to the President of the United States; if he approve he shall sign it, but if not he shall return it, with his Objections to that House in which it shall have originated, who shall enter the Objections at large on their Journal, and proceed to reconsider it. If after such Reconsideration two thirds of that House shall agree to pass the Bill, it shall be sent, together with the Objections, to the other House, by which it shall likewise be reconsidered, and if approved by two thirds of that House, it shall become a Law. But in all such Cases the Votes of both Houses shall be determined by yeas and Nays, and the Names of the Persons voting for and against the Bill shall be entered on the Journal of each House respectively. If any Bill shall not be returned by the President within ten Days (Sundays excepted) after it shall have been presented to him, the Same shall be a Law, in like Manner as if he had signed it, unless the Congress by their Adjournment prevent its Return, in which Case it shall not be a Law.

Every Order, Resolution, or Vote to which the Concurrence of the Senate and House of Representatives may be necessary (except on a question of Adjournment) shall be presented to the President of the United States; and before the Same shall take Effect, shall be approved by him, or being disapproved by him, shall be repassed by two thirds of the Senate and House of Representatives, according to the Rules and Limitations prescribed in the Case of a Bill.

Powers of Congress

Section 8 The Congress shall have Power To lay and collect Taxes, Duties, Imposts and Excises, to pay the Debts and provide for the common Defence and general Welfare of the United States; but all Duties, Imposts and Excises shall be uniform throughout the United States.

To borrow Money on the Credit of the United States;

To regulate Commerce with foreign Nations, and among the several States, and with the Indian Tribes;

To establish an uniform Rule of Naturalization, and uniform Laws on the subject of Bankruptcies throughout the United States;

To coin Money, regulate the Value thereof, and of foreign Coin, and fix the Standard of Weights and Measures;

To provide for the Punishment of counterfeiting the Securities and current Coin of the United States;

To establish Post Offices and post Roads;

To promote the Progress of Science and useful Arts, by securing for limited Times to Authors and Inventors the exclusive Right to their respective Writings and Discoveries;

To constitute Tribunals inferior to the supreme Court;

To define and punish Piracies and Felonies committed on the high Seas, and Offences against the Law of Nations;

To declare War, grant Letters of Marque and Reprisal, and make Rules concerning Captures on Land and Water;

To raise and support Armies, but no Appropriation of Money to that Use shall be for a longer Term than two Years;

To provide and maintain a Navy;

To make Rules for the Government and Regulation of the land and naval Forces;

To provide for calling for the Militia to execute the Laws of the Union, suppress Insurrections and repel Invasions;

To provide for organizing, arming, and disciplining, the Militia, and for governing such Part of them as may be employed in the Service of the United States, reserving to the States respectively, the Appointment of the Officers, and the Authority of training the Militia according to the discipline prescribed by Congress;

To exercise exclusive Legislation in all Cases whatsoever, over such District (not exceeding ten Miles square) as may, by Cession of particular States, and the Acceptance of Congress, become the Seat of the Government of the United States, and to exercise like Authority over all Places purchased by the Consent of the Legislature of the State in which the Same shall be, for the Erection of Forts, Magazines, Arsenals, dock-Yards, and other needful Buildings;—And

To make all Laws which shall be necessary and proper for carrying into Execution the foregoing Powers, and all other Powers vested by this Constitution in the Government of the United States, or in any Department or Officer thereof.

Powers Denied to Congress

Section 9 The Migration of Importation of such Persons as any of the States now existing shall think proper to admit, shall not be prohibited by the Congress prior to the Year one thousand eight hundred and eight, but a Tax or Duty may be imposed on such Importation, not exceeding ten dollars for each Person.

The privilege of the Writ of Habeas Corpus shall not be suspended, unless when in Cases of Rebellion or Invasion the public Safety may require it.

No Bill of Attainder or ex post facto Laws shall be passed.

No Capitation, or other direct, Tax shall be laid, unless in Proportion to the Census or Enumeration herein before directed to be taken.[6]

No Tax or Duty shall be laid on Articles exported from any State.

No Preference shall be given by any Regulation of Commerce or Revenue to the Ports of one State over those of another; nor shall Vessels bound to, or from, one State, be obliged to enter, clear, or pay Duties in another.

No Money shall be drawn from the Treasury, but in Consequence of Appropriations made by Law; and a regular Statement and Account of the Receipts and Expenditures of all public Money shall be published from time to time.

No Title of Nobility shall be granted by the United States; And no Person holding any Office of Profit or Trust under them, shall, without the Consent of Congress, accept of any present, Emolument, Office, or Title, of any kind whatever, from any King, Prince, or foreign State.

Powers Denied to the States

Section 10 No State shall enter into any Treaty, Alliance, or Confederation; grant Letters of Marque and Reprisal; coin Money; emit Bills of Credit; make any Thing but gold and silver Coin a Tender in Payment of Debts; pass any Bill of Attainder, ex post facto Law, or Law impairing the Obligation of Contracts, or grant any Title of Nobility.

No State shall, without the Consent of the Congress, lay any Imposts or Duties on Imports or Exports, except what may be absolutely necessary for executing its inspection Laws: and the net Produce of all Duties and Imposts, laid by any State on Imports or Exports, shall be for the Use of the Treasury of the United States; and all such Laws shall be subject to the Revision and Controul of the Congress.

No State shall, without the Consent of Congress, lay any Duty of Tonnage, keep Troops, or Ships of War in time of Peace, enter into any Agreement or Compact with another State, or with a foreign Power, or engage in War, unless actually invaded, or in such imminent Danger as will not admit of Delay.

ARTICLE II—THE EXECUTIVE ARTICLE

Nature and Scope of Presidential Power

Section 1 The executive Power shall be vested in a President of the United States of America. He shall hold his Office during the Term of four Years and, together with the Vice President, chosen for the same Term, be elected as follows:

Each State shall appoint, in such Manner as the Legislature thereof may direct, a Number of Electors, equal to the whole Number of Senators and Representatives to

---

[6]Modified by the 16th Amendment

which the State may be entitled in the Congress: but no Senator or Representative, or Person holding an Office of Trust or Profit under the United States, shall be appointed an Elector.

The Electors shall meet in their respective States, and vote by Ballot for two Persons, of whom one at least shall not be an Inhabitant of the same State with themselves. And they shall make a List of all the Persons voted for, and of the Number of Votes for each; which List they shall sign and certify, and transmit sealed to the Seat of the Government of the United States, directed to the President of the Senate. The President of the Senate shall, in the Presence of the Senate and House of Representatives, open all the Certificates, and the Votes shall then be counted. The Person having the greatest Number of Votes shall be the President, if such Number be a Majority of the whole Number of Electors appointed; and if there be more than one who have such Majority and have an equal Number of Votes, then the House of Representatives shall immediately chuse by Ballot one of them for President; and if no person have a Majority, then from the five highest on the List the said House shall in like Manner chuse the President. But in chusing the President, the Votes shall be taken by States, the Representation from each State having one Vote; A quorum for this Purpose shall consist of a Member or Members from two thirds of the States, and a Majority of all the States shall be necessary to a Choice. In every Case, after the Choice of the President, the person having the greatest Number of Votes of the Electors shall be the Vice President. But if there should remain two or more who have equal Vote, the Senate shall chuse from them by Ballot the Vice President.[7]

The Congress may determine the Time of chusing the Electors, and the Day on which they shall give their Votes; which Day shall be the same throughout the United States.

No Person except a natural born Citizen, or a Citizen of the United States, at the time of the Adoption of this Constitution, shall be eligible to the Office of President; neither shall any Person be eligible to that Office who shall not have attained to the Age of thirty five Years, and been fourteen Years a Resident within the United States.

In Case of the Removal of the President from Office, or of his Death, Resignation, or Inability to discharge the Powers and Duties of the said Office, the same shall devolve on the Vice President, and the Congress may by Law provide for the Case of Removal, Death, Resignation, or Inability, both of the President and Vice President, declaring what Officer shall then act as President, and such Officer shall act accordingly, until the Disability be removed, or a President shall be elected.[8]

The President shall, at stated Times, receive for his Services, a Compensation, which shall neither be encreased nor diminished during the Period of which he shall have been elected, and he shall not receive within that Period any other Emolument from the United States, or any of them.

Before he enter on the Execution of his Office, he shall take the following Oath

---

[7]Changed by the 12th and 20th Amendments
[8]Modified by the 25th Amendment

or Affirmation:—"I do solemnly swear (or affirm) that I will faithfully execute the Office of President of the United States, and will to the best of my Ability, preserve, protect and defend the Constitution of the United States."

Powers and Duties of the President

Section 2 The President shall be the Commander in Chief of the Army and Navy of the United States, and of the Militia of the several States, when called into the actual Service of the United States, he may require the Opinion, in writing, of the principal Officer in each of the executive Departments, upon any Subject relating to the Duties of their respective Offices, and he shall have the Power to grant Reprieves and Pardons for Offences against the United States, except in Cases of Impeachment.

He shall have Power, by and with the Advice and Consent of the Senate to make Treaties, provided two thirds of the Senators present concur; and he shall nominate, and by and with the Advice and Consent of the Senate, shall appoint Ambassadors, other public Ministers and Consuls, Judges of the supreme Court, and all other Officers of the United States, whose Appointments are not herein otherwise provided for, and which shall be established by Law: but the Congress may by Law vest the Appointment of such inferior Officers, as they think proper, in the President alone, in the Courts of Law, or in the Heads of Departments.

The President shall have Power to fill up all Vacancies that may happen during the Recess of the Senate, by granting Commissions which shall expire at the End of their next Session.

Section 3 He shall from time to time give to the Congress Information of the State of the Union, and recommend to their Consideration such Measures as he shall judge necessary and expedient; he may, on extraordinary Occasions, convene both Houses, or either of them, and in Case of Disagreement between them, with Respect to the Time of Adjournment, he may adjourn them to such Time as he shall think proper; he shall receive Ambassadors and other public Ministers; he shall take Care that the Laws be faithfully executed, and shall Commission all the Officers of the United States.

Section 4 The President, Vice President and all civil Officers of the United States, shall be removed from Office on Impeachment for, and Conviction of, Treason, Bribery, or other High Crimes and Misdemeanors.

Article III—The Judical Article

Judicial Power, Courts, Judges

Section 1 The judicial Power of the United States, shall be vested in one supreme Court, and in such inferior Courts as the Congress may from time to time ordain and establish. The Judges, both the supreme and inferior Courts, shall hold their Offices during good Behaviour, and shall, at stated Times, receive for their Services, a Compensation, which shall not be diminished during their Continuance in Office.

Jurisdiction

Section 2 The judicial Power shall extend to all Cases, in Law and Equity, arising under this Constitution, the Laws of the United States, and Treaties made, or which shall be made, under their Authority;—to all Cases affecting Ambassadors, other public Ministers and Consuls;—to all Cases of admiralty and maritime Jurisdiction;—to Controversies to which the United States shall be a Party;—to Controversies between two or more States; *between a State and Citizens of another State;*[9]— between Citizens of different States;—between Citizens of the same State claiming Lands under Grants of different States, and between a State, or the Citizens thereof, and foreign States, Citizens, or Subjects.

In all Cases affecting Ambassadors, other public Ministers and Consuls, and those in which a State shall be Party, the supreme Court shall have original Jurisdiction. In all the other Cases before mentioned, the supreme Court shall have appellate Jurisdiction, both as to Law and Fact, with such Exceptions, and under such Regulations as Congress shall make.

The Trial of all Crimes, except in Cases of Impeachment, shall be by Jury; and such Trial shall be held in the State where the said Crimes shall have been committed; but when not committed within any State, the Trial shall be at such Place or Places as the Congress may by Law have directed.

Treason

Section 3 Treason against the United States, shall consist only in levying War against them, or in adhering to their Enemies, giving them Aid and Comfort. No Persons shall be convicted of Treason unless on the Testimony of two Witnesses to the same overt Act, or on Confession in open Court.

The Congress shall have Power to declare the Punishment of Treason, but no Attainder of Treason shall work Corruption of Blood, or Forfeiture except during the Life of the Person attainted.

ARTICLE IV—INTERSTATE RELATIONS

Full Faith and Credit Clause

Section 1 Full Faith and Credit shall be given in each State to the public Acts, Records, and judicial Proceedings of every other State. And the Congress may by general Laws prescribe the Manner in which such Acts, Records and Proceedings shall be proved, and the Effect thereof.

---

[9]Modified by the 11th Amendment

Privileges and Immunities; Interstate Extradition

Section 2 The Citizens of each State shall be entitled to all Privileges and Immunities of Citizens in the several States.

A person charged in any State with Treason, Felony or other Crime, who shall flee from Justice, and be found in another State, shall on Demand of the executive Authority of the State from which he fled, be delivered up, to be removed to the State having jurisdiction of the Crime.

No person held to Service or Labour in one State, under the Laws thereof, escaping into another, shall, in Consequence of any Law or Regulation therein, be discharged from such Service or Labour, but shall be delivered up on Claim of the Party to whom such Service or Labour may be due.[10]

Admission of States

Section 3 New States may be admitted by the Congress into this Union; but no new State shall be formed or erected within the Jurisdiction of any other State; nor any State to be formed by the Junction of two or more States, or Parts of States, without the Consent of the Legislatures of the States concerned as well as of the Congress.

The Congress shall have Power to dispose of and make all needful Rules and Regulations respecting the Territory or other Property belonging to the United States; and nothing in this Constitution shall be so construed as to Prejudice any Claims of the United States, or of any particular State.

Republican Form of Government

Section 4 The United States shall guarantee to every State in this Union a Republican Form of Government, and shall protect each of them against Invasion; and on Application of the Legislature, or of the Executive (when the Legislature cannot be convened) against domestic Violence.

ARTICLE V—THE AMENDING POWER

The Congress, whenever two thirds of both Houses shall deem it necessary, shall propose Amendments to this Constitution, or, on the Application of the Legislatures of two thirds of several States, shall call a Convention for proposing Amendments, which, in either Case, shall be valid to all Intents and Purposes, as Part of this Constitution, when ratified by the Legislatures of three fourths of the several States, or by Conventions in three fourths thereof, as the one or the other Mode of Ratification may be proposed by the Congress; Provided that no Amendment which may be made prior to the Year One thousand eight hundred and eight shall in any Manner affect

---

[10]Repealed by the 13th Amendment

the first and fourth Clauses in the Ninth Section of the first Article; and that no State, without its Consent, shall be deprived of its equal Suffrage in the Senate.

ARTICLE VI—THE SUPREMACY ACT

All Debts contracted and Engagements entered into, before the Adoption of this Constitution, shall be as valid against the United States under the Constitution, as under the Confederation.

This Constitution, and the Laws of the United States which shall be made in Pursuance thereof; and all Treaties made, or which shall be made, under the Authority of the United States, shall be the supreme Law of the Land; and the Judges in every State shall be bound thereby, any Thing in the Constitution or Laws of any State to the Contrary notwithstanding.

The Senators and Representatives before mentioned, and the Members of the several State Legislatures, and all executive and judicial Officers, both of the United States and of the several States, shall be bound by Oath or Affirmation, to support this Constitution; but no religious Test shall ever be required as a Qualification to any Office or public Trust under the United States.

ARTICLE VII—RATIFICATION

The Ratification of the Conventions of nine States, shall be sufficient for the Establishment of this Constitution between the States so ratifying the Same.

Done in Convention by the Unanimous Consent of the States present the Seventeenth Day of September in the Year of our Lord one thousand seven hundred and Eighty seven and of the Independence of the United States of America the Twelfth *In Witness whereof We have hereunto subscribed our Names.*

AMENDMENTS

The Bill of Rights

[The first ten amendments were ratified on December 15, 1791, and form what is known as the "Bill of Rights."]

AMENDMENT 1—RELIGION, SPEECH, ASSEMBLY, AND POLITICS

Congress shall make no law respecting an establishment of religion, or prohibiting the free exercise thereof; or abridging the freedom of speech, or of the press; or the right of the people peaceably to assemble, and to petition the government for a redress of grievances.

AMENDMENT 2—MILITIA AND THE RIGHT TO BEAR ARMS

A well regulated Militia, being necessary to the security of a free State, the right of the people to keep and bear Arms, shall not be infringed.

AMENDMENT 3—QUARTERING OF SOLDIERS

No Soldier shall, in time of peace be quartered in any house, without the consent of the Owner, nor in time of war, but in manner to be prescribed by law.

AMENDMENT 4—SEARCHES AND SEIZURES

The right of the people to be secure in their persons, houses, papers, and effects, against unreasonable searches and seizures, shall not be violated, and no Warrants shall issue, but upon probable cause, supported by Oath or affirmation, and particularly describing the place to be searched, and the persons or things to be seized.

AMENDMENT 5—GRAND JURIES, SELF-INCRIMINATION, DOUBLE JEOPARDY, DUE PROCESS, AND EMINENT DOMAIN

No person shall be held to answer for a capital, or otherwise infamous crime, unless on a presentment or indictment of a Grand jury, except in cases arising in the land or naval forces, or in the Militia, when in actual service in time of War or public danger; nor shall any person be subject for the same offence to be twice put in jeopardy of life or limb; nor shall be compelled in any criminal case to be a witness against himself, nor be deprived of life, liberty, or property, without due process of law; nor shall private property be taken for public use, without just compensation.

AMENDMENT 6—CRIMINAL COURT PROCEDURES

In all criminal prosecutions, the accused shall enjoy the right to a speedy and public trial, by an impartial jury of the State and district wherein the crime shall have been committed, which district shall have been previously ascertained by law, and to be informed of the nature and cause of the accusation; to be confronted with the witnesses against him; to have compulsory process for obtaining Witnesses in his favor, and to have the Assistance of Counsel for his defense.

AMENDMENT 7—TRIAL BY JURY IN COMMON LAW CASES

In Suits at common law, where the value in controversy shall exceed twenty dollars, the right of trial by jury shall be preserved, and no fact tried by a jury shall be otherwise re-examined in any Court of the United States, than according to the rules of the common law.

AMENDMENT 8—BAIL, CRUEL AND UNUSUAL PUNISHMENT

Excessive bail shall not be required, nor excessive fines imposed, nor cruel and unusual punishments inflicted.

AMENDMENT 9—RIGHTS RETAINED BY THE PEOPLE

The enumeration in the Constitution, of certain rights, shall not be construed to deny or disparage others retained by the people.

AMENDMENT 10—RESERVED POWERS OF THE STATES

The powers not delegated to the United States by the Constitution, nor prohibited by it to the States, are reserved to the States respectively, or to the people.

AMENDMENT 11—SUITS AGAINST THE STATES
[Ratified February 7, 1795]

The Judicial power of the United States shall not be construed to extend to any suit in law or equity, commenced or prosecuted against one of the United States by Citizens of another State, or by Citizens or Subjects of any Foreign State.

AMENDMENT 12—ELECTION OF THE PRESIDENT
[Ratified June 15, 1804]

The Electors shall meet in their respective states, and vote by ballot for President and Vice-President, one of whom, at least, shall not be an inhabitant of the same state with themselves; they shall name in their ballots the person voted for as President, and in distinct ballots the person voted for as Vice-President, and they shall make distinct lists of all persons voted for as President, and of all persons voted for as Vice-President, and of the number of votes for each, which lists they shall sign and certify, and transmit sealed to the seat of the government of the United States, directed to the President of the Senate;—The President of the Senate shall, in presence of the Senate and House of Representatives, open all the certificates and the votes shall then be counted;—The person having the greatest number of votes for President, shall be the President, if such number be a majority of the whole number of Electors appointed; and if no person have such majority, then from the persons having the highest numbers not exceeding three on the list of those voted for as President, the House of Representatives shall choose immediately, by ballot, the President. But in choosing the President, the votes shall be taken by states, the representation from each state having one vote; a quorum for this purpose shall consist of a member or members from two-thirds of the states, and a majority of all states shall be necessary to a choice. And if the House of Representatives shall not choose a President whenever the right of choice shall devolve upon them, *before the fourth day of March next following,* then the Vice-President shall act as President, as in the case of the death or other constitutional disability of the President.[11] The person having the greatest number of votes as Vice-President, shall be the Vice-President, if such a number be a majority of the whole numbers of Electors appointed, and if no person have a majority, then from the two highest numbers on the list, the Senate shall choose the Vice-President; a quorum for the purpose shall consist of two-thirds of the whole number of Senators, and a majority of the whole number shall be necessary to a choice. But no person constitutionally ineligible to the office of President shall be eligible to that of Vice-President of the United States.

AMENDMENT 13—PROHIBITION OF SLAVERY
[Ratified December 6, 1865]

Section 1 Neither slavery nor involuntary servitude, except as a punishment for crime whereof the party shall have been duly convicted, shall exist within the United States, or any place subject to their jurisdiction.

Section 2 Congress shall have power to enforce this article by appropriate leg-islation.

AMENDMENT 14—CITIZENSHIP, DUE PROCESS, AND EQUAL PROTECTION OF THE LAWS
[Ratified July 9, 1868]

Section 1 All persons born or naturalized in the United States, and subject to the jurisdiction thereof, are citizens of the United States and of the State wherein they reside. No State shall make or enforce any law which shall abridge the privileges or immunities of citizens of the United States; nor shall any State deprive any person of life, liberty, or property, without due process of law; nor deny to any person within its jurisdiction the equal protection of the laws.

Section 2 Representatives shall be apportioned among the several States according to their respective numbers, counting the whole number of persons in each State, excluding Indians not taxed. But when the right to vote at any election for the choice of electors for President and Vice President of the United States, Representatives in Congress, the Executive and Judicial officers of a State, or the members of the Legislature thereof, is denied to any of the male inhabitants of such State, being twenty-one[12] years of age, and citizens of the United States, or in any way abridged, except for participation in rebellion, or

---

[11]Changed by the 20th Amendment
[12]Changed by the 26th Amendment

other crime, the basis of representation therein shall be reduced in the proportion which the number of such male citizens shall bear to the whole number of male citizens twenty-one years of age in such State.

Section 3 No person shall be a Senator or Representative in Congress, or elector of President and Vice President, or hold any office, civil or military, under the United States, or under any State, who, having previously taken an oath, as a member of Congress, or as an officer of the United States, or as a member of any State legislature, or as an executive or judicial officer of any State, to support the Constitution of the United States, shall have engaged in insurrection or rebellion against the same, or given aid or comfort to the enemies thereof. But Congress may by a vote of two-thirds of each House, remove such disability.

Section 4 The validity of the public debt of the United States, authorized by law, including debts incurred for payment of pensions and bounties for services in suppressing insurrection or rebellion, shall not be questioned. But neither the United States nor any State shall assume or pay any debt or obligation incurred in aid of insurrection or rebellion against the United States, or any claim for the loss or emancipation of any slave; but all such debts, obligations and claims shall be held illegal and void.

Section 5 The Congress shall have power to enforce, by appropriate legislation, the provisions of this article.

AMENDMENT 15—THE RIGHT TO VOTE
[Ratified February 3, 1870]

Section 1 The right of citizens of the United States to vote shall not be denied or abridged by the United States or by any State on account of race, color, or previous condition of servitude.

Section 2 The Congress shall have power to enforce this article by appropriate legislation.

AMENDMENT 16—INCOME TAXES
[Ratified February 3, 1913]

The Congress shall have power to lay and collect taxes on incomes, from whatever source derived, without apportionment among the several States, and without regard to any census or enumeration.

AMENDMENT 17—DIRECT ELECTION OF SENATORS
[Ratified April 8, 1913]

The Senate of the United States shall be composed of two Senators from each State, elected by the people thereof, for six years; and each Senator shall have one vote. The electors in each State shall have the qualifications requisite for electors of the most numerous branch of the State legislatures.

When vacancies happen in the representation of any State in the Senate, the executive authority of such State shall issue writs of election to fill such vacancies: *Provided*, That the Legislature of any State may empower the executive thereof to make temporary appointment until the people fill the vacancies by election as the legislature may direct.

This amendment shall not be so construed as to affect the election or term of any Senator chosen before it becomes valid as part of the Constitution.

AMENDMENT 18—PROHIBITION
[Ratified January 16, 1919. Repealed December 5, 1933 by Amendment 21]

Section 1 After one year from the ratification of this article the manufacture, sale, or transportation of intoxicating liquors within, the importation thereof into, or the exportation thereof from the United States and all territory subject to the jurisdiction thereof for beverage purposes is hereby prohibited.

Section 2 The Congress and the several states shall have concurrent power to enforce this article by appropriate legislation.

Section 3 This article shall be inoperative unless it shall have been ratified as an amendment to the Constitution by the legislatures of the several states, as provided in the Constitution, within seven years from the date of the submission hereof to the States by the Congress.[13]

AMENDMENT 19—FOR WOMEN'S SUFFRAGE
[Ratified August 18, 1920]

The right of the citizens of the United States to vote shall not be denied or abridged by the United States or by any State on account of sex.

Congress shall have power, by appropriate legislation, to enforce the provision of this article.

AMENDMENT 20—THE LAME DUCK AMENDMENT
[Ratified January 23, 1933]

Section 1 The terms of the President and Vice President shall end at noon on the 20th day of January, and the terms of the Senators and Representatives at noon on the 3rd day of January, of the years in which such terms would have ended if this article had not been ratified; and the terms of their successors shall then begin.

---

[13]Repealed by the 21st Amendment

Section 2 The Congress shall assemble at least once in every year, and such meeting shall begin at noon on the 3rd day of January, unless they shall by law appoint a different day.

Section 3 If, at the time fixed for the beginning of the term of the President, the President elect shall have died, the Vice President elect shall become President. If a President shall not have been chosen before the time fixed for the beginning of his term, or if the President elect shall have failed to qualify, then the Vice President elect shall act as President until a President shall have qualified; and the Congress may by law provide for the case wherein neither a President elect nor a Vice President elect shall have qualified, declaring who shall then act as President, or the manner in which one who is to act shall be selected, and such person shall act accordingly until a President or Vice President shall have qualified.

Section 4 The Congress may by law provide for the case of the death of any of the persons from whom the House of Representatives may choose a President whenever the right of choice shall have developed upon them, and for the case of the death of any of the persons from whom the Senate may choose a Vice President whenever the right of choice shall have devolved upon them.

Section 5 Sections 1 and 2 shall take effect on the 15th day of October following the ratification of this article.

Section 6 This article shall be inoperative unless it shall have been ratified as an amendment to the Constitution by the legislatures of three-fourths of the several States within seven years from the date of its submission.

AMENDMENT 21—REPEAL OF PROHIBITION
[Ratified December 5, 1933]

Section 1 The eighteenth article of amendment to the Constitution of the United States is hereby repealed.

Section 2 The transportation or importation into any State, Territory, or Possession of the United States for delivery or use therein of intoxicating liquors, in violation of the laws thereof, is hereby prohibited.

Section 3 This article shall be inoperative unless it shall have been ratified as an amendment to the Constitution by conventions in the several States, as provided in the Constitution, within seven years from the date of the submission hereof to the States by the Congress.

AMENDMENT 22—NUMBER OF PRESIDENTIAL TERMS
[Ratified February 27, 1951]

Section 1 No person shall be elected to the office of the President more than twice, and no person who has held the office of President, or acted as President, for more than two years of a term to which some other person was elected President shall be elected to the Office of the President more than once. But this Article shall not apply to any person holding the office of President when this article was proposed by the Congress, and shall not prevent any person who may be holding the office of President, or acting as President, during the term within which this Article becomes operative from holding the office of President or acting as President during the remainder of such term.

Section 2 This Article shall be inoperative unless it shall have been ratified as an amendment to the Constitution by the legislatures of three-fourths of the several states within seven years from the date of its submission to the States by the Congress.

AMENDMENT 23—PRESIDENTIAL ELECTORS FOR THE DISTRICT OF COLUMBIA
[Ratified March 29, 1961]

Section 1 The District constituting the seat of Government of the United States shall appoint in such manner as the Congress may direct:

A number of electors of President and Vice President equal to the whole number of Senators and Representatives in Congress to which the District would be entitled if it were a State, but in no event more than the least populous State; they shall be in addition to those appointed by the States, but they shall be considered, for the purposes of the election of President and Vice President, to be electors appointed by a State; and they shall meet in the District and perform such duties as provided by the twelfth article of amendment.

Section 2 The Congress shall have power to enforce this article by appropriate legislation.

AMENDMENT 24—THE ANTI-POLL TAX AMENDMENT
[Ratified January 23, 1964]

Section 1 The right of citizens of the United States to vote in any primary or other election for President or Vice President, for electors for President or Vice President, or for Senator or Representative in Congress, shall not be denied or abridged by the United States or any State by reason of failure to pay any poll tax or other tax.

Section 2 The Congress shall have power to enforce this article by appropriate legislation.

AMENDMENT 25—PRESIDENTIAL DISABILITY, VICE PRESIDENTIAL VACANCIES
[Ratified February 10, 1967]

Section 1 In case of the removal of the President from office or his death or resignation, the Vice President shall become President.

Section 2 Whenever there is a vacancy in the office of the Vice President, the President shall nominate a Vice President who shall take the office upon confirmation by a majority vote of both houses of Congress.

Section 3 Whenever the President transmits to the President pro tempore of the Senate and the Speaker of the House of Representatives his written declaration that he is unable to discharge the powers and duties of his office, and until he transmits to them a written declaration to the contrary, such powers and duties shall be discharged by the Vice President as Acting President.

Section 4 Whenever the Vice-President and a majority of either the principal officers of the executive departments, or of such other body as Congress may by law provide, transmit to the President pro tempore of the Senate and the Speaker of the House of Representatives their written declaration that the President is unable to discharge the powers and duties of his office, the Vice President shall immediately assume the powers and duties of the office as Acting President.

Thereafter, when the President transmits to the President pro tempore of the Senate and the Speaker of the House of Representatives his written declaration that no inability exists, he shall resume the powers and duties of his office unless the Vice President and a majority of either the principal officers of the executive departments, or of such other body as Congress may by law provide, transmit within four days to the President pro tempore of the Senate and the Speaker of the House of Representatives their written declaration that the President is unable to discharge the powers and duties of his office. Thereupon Congress shall decide the issue, assembling within forty-eight hours for that purpose if not in session. If the Congress, within twenty-one days after receipt of the latter written declaration, or, if Congress is not in session, within twenty-one days after Congress is required to assemble, determines by two-thirds vote of both houses that the President is unable to discharge the powers and duties of his office, the Vice President shall continue to discharge the same as Acting President; otherwise, the President shall resume the powers and duties of his office.

AMENDMENT 26—EIGHTEEN-YEAR-OLD VOTE
[Ratified July 1, 1971]

Section 1 The right of citizens of the United States, who are eighteen years of age, or older, to vote shall not be denied or abridged by the United States or by any State on account of age.

Section 2 The Congress shall have power to enforce this article by appropriate legislation.

AMENDMENT 27—CONGRESSIONAL SALARIES
[Ratified May 7, 1992]

No law, varying the compensation for the services of the Senators and Representatives, shall take effect, until an election of Representative shall be intervened.

APPENDIX B

Case List

GENERAL

Baker v. Carr 369 US 186 (1962)
Brown v. Allen 344 US 443 (1953)
Cherokee Cases 30 US 1 (1831), 31 US 515 (1832)
Chisholm v. Georgia 2 US 419 (1793)
CTS Corp. v. Dynamics Corp. 481 US 69 (1987)
DeShaney v. Winnebago Cty. Soc. Servs. Dept. 489 US 189 (1989)
Flood v. Kuhn 407 US 258 (1972)
Immigration and Naturalization Service v. Chadha 462 US 919 (1983)
Landgraf v. USI Film Products 128 LEd2d 229 (1994)
Marbury v. Madison 5 US 137 (1803)
National Labor Relations Board v. Jones & Laughlin Steel Corp. 301 US 1 (1937)
New State Ice Co, v. Liebmann 285 US 262 (1932)
Oregon v. Mitchell 400 US 112 (1970)
Pollock v. Farmer's Loan and Trust Co. 157 US 429 (1895)
San Antonio School District v. Rodriguez 411 US 1 (1973)
U.S. v. Lopez 115 SCt 1624 (1995)
U.S. v. Nixon 418 US 683 (1974)
U.S. v. Robertson No. 94-251 (1995)
U.S. Term Limits, Inc. v. Thornton 115 SCt1842 (1995)
West Virginia State Board of Education v. Barnette 319 US 624 (1943)

GENDER

General, Title IX, Sexual Harassment

Bradwell v. Illinois 83 US 130 (1873)
California Federal Savings & Loan v. Guerra 479 US 272 (1987)
Cleveland Board of Education v. LaFleuer 414 US 632 (1974)
Franklin v. Gwinnett Cty Pub Schools 117 LEd2d 208 (1992)
Frontiero v. Richardson 411 US 677 (1973)
Geduldig v. Aiello 417 US 484 (1974)
General Electric Co. v. Gilbert 429 US 124 (1976)
Goesaert v. Cleary 335 US 464 (1948)
Grove City College v. Bell 465 US 555 (1984)
Harris v. Forklift Systems 126 LEd2d 295 (1993)
Hoyt v. Florida 368 US 57 (1961)
International Union v. Johnson Controls, Inc. 111 SCt 1196 (1991)
Johnson v. Santa Clara County 480 US 616 (1987)
Los Angeles Dept. of Water and Power v. Manhart 435 US 702 (1978)
Meritor Savings Bank v. Vinson 477 US 57 (1986)
Minor v. Happersett 88 US 162 (1875)
Mississippi University for Women v. Hogan 458 US 718 (1982)
Muller v. Oregon 208 US 412 (1908)
Newport News Shipbuilding & Dry Dock Co. v. EEOC 462 US 669 (1983)
Price Waterhouse v. Hopkins 490 US 228 (1989)
Reed v. Reed 404 US 71 (1971)

PRIVACY

Bowers v. Hardwick 478 US 186 (1986)
Griswold v. Connecticut 381 US 479 (1965)
Moore v. City of East Cleveland 431 US 494 (1977)
Stanley v. Georgia 394 US 557 (1969)

PRIVACY

Abortion

Harris v. McRae 448 US 297 (1980)
NOW v. Scheidler 127 LEd2d 99 (1994)
Roe v. Wade 410 US 113 (1973)
Rust v. Sullivan 111 SCt 1759 (1991)

RACE

Bolling v. Sharpe 347 US 497 (1954)
Brown v. Board of Education 347 US 483 (1954)
Brown v. Board of Education 349 US 294 (1955)
Cooper v. Aaron 358 US 1 (1958)
Green v. County School Board 391 US 430 (1968)
Griggs v. Duke Power Co. 401 US 424 (1971)
Heart of Atlanta Motel v. US 379 US 241 (1964)
Katzenbach v. McClung 379 US 294 (1964)
Loving v. Virginia 388 US 1 (1967)
Palmer v. Thompson 403 US 217 (1971)
Regents of the University of California v. Bakke 438 US 265 (1978)
Scott v. Sandford 60 US 393 (1857)
United Steel Workers of America v. Weber 443 US 193 (1979)
Wygant v. Jackson Board of Education 476 US 267 (1986)

RELIGION

Abington School Dist. v. Schempp 374 US 203 (1963)
Capitol Square Review Bd. v. Pinette No. 94-780 (1995)
Church of the Lukumi Babalu Aye, Inc. v. Hialeah 124 LEd2d 472 (1993)
Edwards v. Aguillard 482 US 578 (1987)
Employment Division v. Smith 494 US 872 (1990)
Engel v. Vitale 370 US 421 (1962)
Lee v. Weisman 112 SCt 2649 (1992)
Lemon v. Kurtzman 403 US 602 (1971)
Lynch v. Donnelly 465 US 668 (1984)
Rosenberger v. University of Virginia No. 94-329 (1995)
Sherbert v. Verner 374 US 398 (1963)
Stone v. Graham 449 US 539 (1980)
Wallace v. Jaffree 472 US 38 (1985)
Westside Community Board of Education v. Mergens 496 US 226 (1990)
Widmar v. Vincent 454 US 263 (1981)
Wisconsin v. Yoder 406 US 205 (1972)

SPEECH

Brandenburg v. Ohio 395 US 444 (1969)
Chaplinsky v. New Hampshire 315 US 568 (1942)
Cohen v. California 403 US 15 (1971)
Cox v. Louisiana 379 US 536 (1965)

New York Times Co. v. Sullivan 376 US 254 (1964)
R.A.V. v. St. Paul 120 LEd2d 305 (1992)
Simon and Schuster v. Crime Victims Board 116 LEd2d 476 (1991)
Texas v. Johnson 105 LEd2d 342 (1989)
Tinker v. Des Moines 393 US 503 (1969)
U.S. v. Eichman 496 US 310 (1990)
U.S. v. O'Brien 391 US 367 (1968)
Wisconsin v. Mitchell 124 LEd2d 436 (1993)

Obscenity

Barnes v. Glen Theatre 111 SCt 2456 (1991)
FCC v. Pacifica 438 US 726 (1978)
Ginzburg v. US 383 US 463 (1966)
Jacobellis v. Ohio 378 US 184 (1964)
Miller v. California 413 US 15 (1973)
Roth v. US 354 US 476 (1957)
Schad v. Mount Ephraim 452 US 61 (1981)

NON-SUPREME COURT CASES

Cohen v. Brown 879 F.Supp. 185 (1995)
State v. Henry 732 P.2d 9 (OR 1987)
U.S. v. Bishop 94-5321 (1995)

Bibliography/Suggested Reading

Alderman, E. and Kennedy, C., *In Our Defense, The Bill of Rights in Action*. New York: Avon Books, 1991.

Brill, A., *Nobody's Business: The Paradoxes of Privacy*. Reading, MA: Addison-Wesley, 1990.

Carruth, G., *What Happened When: A Chronology of Life & Events in America*. New York: Signet Books, 1991.

Carter, S. L., *Reflections of an Affirmative Action Baby*. New York: BasicBooks, 1991.

Carter, S. L., *The Culture of Disbelief: How American Law and Politics Trivialize Religious Devotion*. New York: Doubleday, 1993

Carter, S. L., *The Confirmation Mess: Cleaning Up the Federal Appointments Process*. New York: BasicBooks, 1994.

Cox, A., *The Court and the Constitution*. Boston, MA: Houghton Mifflin, 1987.

Davis, M. D. and Clark, H. R., *Thurgood Marshall: A Warrior at the Bar, Rebel on the Bench*. New York: Carol Publishing Group, 1994.

deGrazia, E., *Girls Lean Back Everywhere: The Law of Obscenity and the Assault on Genius*. New York: Vintage Books, 1992.

Dorsen, N., (ed.), *The Evolving Constitution*. Middletown, CT: Wesleyan University Press, 1987.

Ezorsky, G., *Racism and Justice*. Ithaca, NY: Cornell University Press, 1991.

Faludi, S., *Backlash: The Undeclared War Against American Women*. New York: Crown Publishers, 1991.

Glasser, I. and Adelman, B., *Visions of Liberty: The Bill of Rights for All Americans*. New York: Arcade Publishing, 1991.

Greenberg, J., *Crusaders in the Courts: How a Dedicated Band of Lawyers Fought for the Civil Rights Revolution*. New York: BasicBooks, 1994.

Hall, K. L., (ed.), *The Oxford Companion to the Supreme Court.* New York: Oxford University Press, 1992.

Heins, M., *Sex, Sin and Blasphemy: A Guide to America's Censorship Wars.* New York: The New Press, 1993.

Hentoff, N., *Free Speech For Me—But Not For Thee: How the American Left and Right Relentlessly Censor Each Other.* New York: HarperCollins, 1992.

Irons, P. and Guitton, S., (eds.), *May It Please the Court: The Most Significant Oral Arguments Before the Supreme Court Since 1955.* New York: The New Press, 1993.

Kalvan, J., Jr., *A Worthy Tradition: Freedom of Speech in America.* New York: Harper & Row, 1989.

Maltz, E. M., *Rethinking Constitutional Law: Originalism, Interventionism, and the Politics of Judicial Review.* Lawrence: The University Press of Kansas, 1994.

Mayer, J. and Abramson, J., *Strange Justice: The Selling of Clarence Thomas.* New York: Houghton Mifflin, 1994.

O'Neill, W., *Coming Apart: An Informal History of America in the 1960s.* New York: Times Books, 1971.

Patrick, J. J., *The Young Oxford Companion to the Supreme Court of the United States.* New York: Oxford University Press, 1994.

Rowan, C. T., *Dream Makers, Dream Breakers: The World of Justice Thurgood Marshall.* Boston, MA: Little Brown, 1993.

Savage, D. G., *Turning Right: The Making of the Rehnquist Court.* New York: John Wiley, 1993.

Silverstein, M., *Judicious Choices: The New Politics of the Supreme Court Confirmations.* New York: W.W. Norton, 1994.

Simon, J. F., *The Center Holds: The Power Struggle Inside the Rehnquist Court.* New York: Simon & Schuster, 1995.

Strossen, N., *Defending Porn: Free Speech, Sex, and the Fight for Women's Rights.* New York: Scribner, 1995.

Tribe, L. H., *God Save This Honorable Court: How the Choice of Supreme Court Justices Shapes Our History.* New York: Mentor Books, 1985.

Tribe, L. H., *Abortion, The Clash of Absolutes.* New York: W.W. Norton, 1992.

U.S. Attorney General, *Final Report of the Attorney General's Commission on Pornography.* Nashville, TN: Rutledge Hill Press, 1986.

Van Dyke, V., *Equality and Public Policy.* Chicago, IL: Nelson-Hall, 1990.

West, C., *Race Matters.* New York: Vintage Books, 1994.

Witt, E., *The Supreme Court and Individual Rights* (2nd ed.). Washington, DC: Congressional Quarterly, 1988.

Woodward, B. and Armstrong, S., *The Brethren: Inside the Supreme Court.* New York: Simon & Schuster, 1979.

Index